AF266717

Hodgepodge, Mishmash, and Jumble

Ted Ringer

These are a few of my favorite words.

Hodgepodge, Mishmash, and Jumble
Published by Wonderful World Publishing

ISBN: 978-0-9848807-1-3

Cover design by Ted Ringer.

Also by Ted Ringer

Born with a Beard
Gus Goes West
Drawing and Dreaming
The Lure of the Garage
Get Outta Town, a tale of the Grateful Dead, the IRS, and Coffee
Ringer's Secret School of Writing — Semesters One and Two
Tales of the Vampire Hunters
Fit To Love — The Endless Twitter Novel

Paswonky — A music blog —www.paswonky.wordpress.com

For Mary Liz —

Our stars align.
Our hearts agree.
Our place is together.

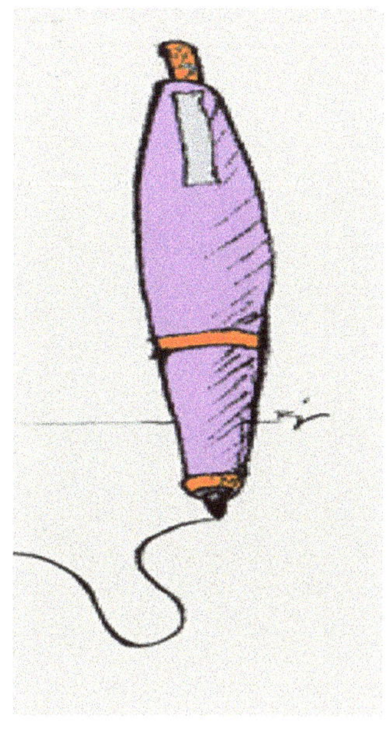

The pen is mightier than the sword
And easier to carry.

Contents

Introduction/Preface/Explanation/Author's Note

This volume collects work from the last fifty years. Holy cow!

A Smattering

Down With Gravity

Deeper Than My Navel

Have you ever had one of those moments where the curtains draw back, the light is blinding, and you are filled with a revelation that you've had before, but it's amazing all the same?

I'm not talking about waking up this morning. I mean a moment of epiphany when, all of a sudden, you are struck dumb by the immensity of it all. The whole thing. The doughnut and the hole. Kind of like your twenty-first birthday, but even bigger. Even bigger than fifty. And, in some cases, bigger than that.

It can happen at any time. One moment, you're going about your day and the next, you look at something and it's as if you're seeing it for the first time. Like King Kong on top of the Empire State Building. Like a satellite moving across the sky. Like a cannonball from the high dive.

I'm talking about the moment you find yourself looking at your hand or arm or something and you are completely floored, because it's actually holding a glass. That it works. That it obeys your will. You raise the glass to your lips, just to be sure. That taste! Those tastebuds! The blood in your veins. The connections in your mind. It all works! Cells reproducing, communicating, your stomach digesting. These very thoughts! What a miracle!

You don't know what to think. You look away and gaze into the backyard. You see flowers, bushes, the grass. How do they do it?! And then, even more profound, Why?!

It is truly a moment of revelation and wonderment. You're suddenly on philosophical overload and everything begins to take on a kind of glow. You lift your eyes to the heavens and begin to contemplate the mysteries of the universe. How is this possible? Who figured all this stuff out? Why are we here?

You turn to your wife. A wonderful innocence shines out of you, as you say, "Have you ever wondered why we're here?" And, she says, "Honey, what about lunch?"

In that moment, you drop back to everyday reality like a stone. These thoughts are so huge, you can't entertain them for long. Not only that, but, put into words, they sound either naïve and pretentious or like it's time you took your medication. It seems only people with special training can deal with these questions — monks, astronauts, and fifth grade teachers.

And yet, it is a miracle. And an ongoing one. In every moment of forever, this has been happening. It has never stopped. Don't even start wondering about the beginning and why, in the first place, all this stuff happened.

Seeing the world in a grain of sand or the miracle of life in the most mundane of occurrences is the kind of thinking that slows you down and warms you, but like the sun, you don't want to look directly at it, for more than a moment.

Special training is not required, but it's better to start out with this as a passing thought that you can contemplate, whenever you like, just not for too long. One that will warm your heart, make you think, and keep things growing.

I always ask myself, what would I do?

www.bumpersticker.guru

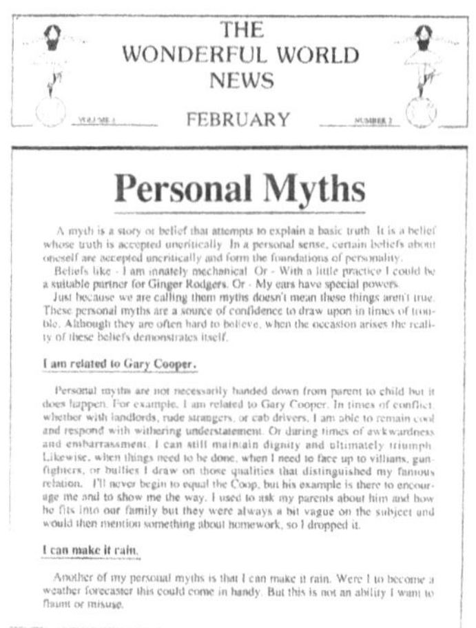

THE WONDERFUL WORLD NEWS

VOLUME 1 — FEBRUARY — NUMBER 2

Personal Myths

A myth is a story or belief that attempts to explain a basic truth. It is a belief whose truth is accepted uncritically. In a personal sense, certain beliefs about oneself are accepted uncritically and form the foundations of personality.

Beliefs like - I am innately mechanical. Or - With a little practice I could be a suitable partner for Ginger Rodgers. Or - My ears have special powers.

Just because we are calling them myths doesn't mean these things aren't true. These personal myths are a source of confidence to draw upon in times of trouble. Although they are often hard to believe, when the occasion arises the reality of these beliefs demonstrates itself.

I am related to Gary Cooper.

Personal myths are not necessarily handed down from parent to child but it does happen. For example, I am related to Gary Cooper. In times of conflict, whether with landlords, rude strangers, or cab drivers, I am able to remain cool and respond with withering understatement. Or during times of awkwardness and embarrassment, I can still maintain dignity and ultimately triumph. Likewise, when things need to be done, when I need to face up to villians, gunfighters, or bullies I draw on those qualities that distinguished my famous relation. I'll never begin to equal the Coop, but his example is there to encourage me and to show me the way. I used to ask my parents about him and how he fits into our family but they were always a bit vague on the subject and would then mention something about homework, so I dropped it.

I can make it rain.

Another of my personal myths is that I can make it rain. Were I to become a weather forecaster this could come in handy. But this is not an ability I want to flaunt or misuse.

Personal Myths

A myth is a story or belief that attempts to explain a basic truth. It is a belief whose truth is accepted uncritically. In a personal sense, certain beliefs about oneself are accepted uncritically and form the foundations of personality. Beliefs like, I am innately mechanical. Or, with a little practice I could be a suitable partner for Ginger Rodgers. Or, my ears have special powers. Just because we are calling them myths doesn't mean these things aren't true. These personal myths are a source of confidence to draw upon in times of trouble. Although they are often hard to believe, when the occasion arises, the reality of these beliefs demonstrates itself.

I am related to Gary Cooper.

Personal myths are not necessarily handed down from parent to child, but it does happen. For example, I am related to Gary Cooper. In times of conflict, whether with landlords, rude strangers, or cab drivers, I am able to remain cool and respond with withering understatement. Or during times of awkwardness and embarrassment, I can still maintain dignity and ultimately triumph.

Likewise, when things need to be done, when I need to face up to villains, gunfighters, or bullies, I draw on those qualities that distinguished my famous relation. I'll never begin to equal the Coop, but his example is there to encourage me and to show me the way. I used to ask my parents about him and how he fits into our family, but they were always a bit vague on the subject and would then mention something about homework, so I dropped it.

I can make it rain.

Another of my personal myths is that I can make it rain. Were I to become a weather forecaster, this could come in handy. But this is not an ability I want to flaunt or misuse. I took my first swimming lessons from a man who was bald. However, he did have curly, white chest hairs and a trident in his left hand. I would go down to the dock at the lake at my grandparent's house and he would rise out of the water, grab me, and throw me in. Then, in a thunderous voice, he would command, " Swim! " Most of the time I made it to shore.

As you can imagine, this was not a pleasant experience and one which I dreaded all week. I decided to make it rain, figuring that by doing this I could avoid the lesson. This was an act of survival. My swimming skills were not improving, as far as I could see, and I was certain that it was only a matter of time before I suffered a watery death that would not only upset myself, but my parents and my grandparents.

I had read about rain dances performed by Indian shamans. And so, on the day of my lesson, I drank the sacred chocolate milk and ate the necessary, not to mention holy, cookies. I went out into the blazing sun in my swimming suit and, as I had seen people do on TV, danced in circles chanting — *"Hoya Hoya — Oogga Oogga."* I took no notice of the neighbors. After two minutes I felt the first drop. Then another. I looked up.

The sky was blue. No clouds. And yet, the rain began to pour down. The lesson was cancelled. I was amazed at my ability to bring this about and believed that if I could do this, I could certainly learn how to swim. Eventually, I did.

Famous people seek me out.

Throughout my life, I have avoided celebrities. I have no idea of what to say to them. I can't picture them doing the dishes or making up a grocery list. The tabloids hold no attraction for me. And yet it seems that the rich, the famous, and the powerful seek me out.

Once, when I was young, I was loitering about a clothing store. Up to the front door glided a long, black, shiny limo and from within it emerged several Secret Servicemen who surrounded a person who turned out to be Hubert Humphrey, then U. S. Senator. At the time, he was a big deal in Minnesota. They entered the store and glided straight up to me. Mr. Humphrey smiled, shook my hand and confidentially told me he was shopping. He then purchased some socks, glided out the door with his friends and was gone.

Another time I was loitering at the airport in Denver and met Jimi Hendrix. I was eating an apple when this especially outlandish guy walked up to me and asked if I had another one. I did and I gave it to him. He said "Thanks, man," and continued on his way.

Later in life, while loitering one night at a bar, I watched a person I knew to be the great jazz bassist Charles Mingus, walk towards me. I calmly drank my beer. He stood next to me and looked me over. Then in a voice that was a cross between a frog's croak and the growl of some large animal, he said, "Don't I know you?" I said, "Of course you do, but we've never met.'

I have a special rapport with animals.

Animals, though animals, are quite sensitive creatures. Behind those mysterious eyes lies a consciousness not that different from our own. Because they do not have to talk on the phone or use public transportation, they are more in touch with their spiritual side.

I'm not sure what it means, but I feel that cows understand me. When I'm in the country and walk up to the fence, they look at me with that special look. There is a communication between us that goes beyond words.

Cats and dogs also are drawn to me. I possess some magic touch that makes them purr and wag their tails. And fish, who usually turn a cold shoulder to most people, will rush right up to me and bite my legs, while I'm learning to swim.

I can gain five lbs. one day and lose it the next.

I'm a meat and potatoes kind of guy. I believe in eating every day from the four basic food groups: Alcohol, Fries, Meat, and Sugar. Vegetables have their place, but it is secondary. For a long time, I considered dessert superfluous but have since broadened my vision of what is necessary to sustain life.

It's amazing. I will sit down to a meal consisting of a huge steak covered with butter, a steaming baked potato the size of a boot covered with butter, a modest portion of broccoli covered with butter, accompanied by a baguette of French (or Italian) bread covered with garlic butter, and a bottle of red wine, followed by a rather large hunk of cheesecake.

The next morning, when I weigh in for the day, I often find that I have gained up to five new pounds. This does not disturb me because I know that I have a metabolism that confounds not only science but common sense as well. By not eating and by working myself into a frenzy, I can lose this newly gained weight by the next morning. Or perhaps the morning after that. Definitely next week. I mean it.

I was born with a beard.

This is not funny. For those of you who don't know me personally, I have a large dark beard which is turning white. I trim it. It grows. I trim it. It has always been this way. I look back through old yearbooks and at old family albums and there I am — not only the tallest in the picture but the one with the longest beard. In fact, the only beard in all these pictures. None of my classmates or teachers had beards. None of my aunts or uncles either.

My parents, bless them, have never made me feel that a beard is something to be ashamed of. I guess seeing it on me from Day One made it a special sign to them of some sort. They did, at one time, get a little upset about my long hair, but you know how it was back then.

I used to ask them if Gary Cooper was born with a beard, but they were always a bit vague on the subject and would then mention something about homework, so I dropped it. Although there have been moments in my past when I felt self-conscious about it, I have come to accept and celebrate this beard as just another part of me, like my toes.

So, you see, like our toes, these personal myths can ground us and support us in a world that is always changing and that we have come to see is always unpredictable. They may seem to others unlikely and more wishful thinking than actual reality, but each of us carries within us our own mythology and that is what makes us the unique individuals that make up this wonderful world.

Conversation Piece

As if we didn't have enough to talk about.

Be Your Own Boss

My sister was very mature for her age. By this, I don't mean she was six feet tall. I mean she knew things. She knew Geography and proved it by teaching me the capitals of all the states. She knew the difference between a Ford and a Chevy. She had developed her powers of observation to a point where it seemed as if she could read my mind.

"Don't look at me that way," she would say.

I thought, "What way?" and then, upon reflection, realize that I had been thinking that her barrette was really in bad taste.

She had acquired a surprising command of the French language and all things French. She would ex-claim, "Mon Dieu!" and was very fond of French fries. She shocked my mother by suggesting, one night, that perhaps at some time in the future we could have frog legs for dinner. Her favorite painters were Edouard Manet and Henri Rousseau, though it may have had something to do with how their names sounded.

She was quite self-possessed and didn't lose her temper or cry much, preferring to adopt a somewhat distant and worldly stance toward the normal trials and tribulations of growing up. She was unlike her friends and classmates in this. They would be fighting over a doll, with earnest tears in their eyes, and she would look at them and comment on the impermanence of childhood. I've seen her do it. I don't mean to suggest that she was cold or inhuman, but just that she had the ability to see things from another perspective.

She had a reservoir of ambition that seemed unique to our family. Her plans for guiding the future of the French state were an example of this. It seemed like she studied all the time. She not only had her nose in a book, it seemed she would crawl right into it entirely. Once she read about leopards and painted spots all over herself and didn't speak or get off of all fours for two days. Mom and Dad tried to reason with her, but she arched her back, hissed threateningly, and took a swipe at them with her paw.

Another example of her unbounded ambition was the mail she received. One day, she started getting stuff in the mail. At first, Mom thought it was some kind of mix-up, but it kept coming. Every few days my sister would receive, addressed to her, a pamphlet which would announce in bold letters — EARN $$$ AT HOME IN YOUR SPARE TIME. BE YOUR OWN BOSS! It would go on to explain how, by stuffing envelopes or something, my sister would soon have enough money to buy a new car.

She was sent information on how to become a locksmith. How to start your own import business. Sharpen lawn mower blades. Start a sawmill. Study interior design. Mechanical drafting. It was endless. Home correspondence school material lined the shelves of our bedroom. She was learning the secrets of the Rosicrucians. She was becoming a veterinarian.

My father thought my sister was a budding businessman and entrepreneur like himself. Mom didn't know what to think. Her daughter a sawmill operator? She finally put her foot down when she saw, among the innocent looking bills, a piece of literature with a headline that blared — DEVELOP A BEAUTIFUL BUST IN ONLY ONE MINUTE A DAY. This was not her idea of the kind of material my sister should possess.

My sister did know the value of a dollar. She would save every cent she could get her hands on. Her eyes were always on the ground, looking for that fumbled penny or that displaced dime. She would do extra chores to add to her horde of coins. She even participated in what, I thought, was a ghoulish practice — selling her teeth.

Maybe it was because I didn't have any teeth. Maybe I just had no understanding and appreciation of tradition. Maybe I wasn't mature enough, but the idea of selling a part of your body, especially one that had been in your mouth, to someone you didn't even know, was one I couldn't grasp. And to a mysterious, supernatural being at that.

What did this Tooth Fairy want them for? What did the Tooth Fairy do with them? I couldn't imagine it, and when my sister told me that the Tooth Fairy takes them from all the kids, I was really concerned. What if you didn't want to give them up? Would he come down one night and extract them?

As I lay in my crib, thinking about this, I had my first misgivings about growing up. It shook me. It also unnerved me to see the lengths to which my sister would go to get the Fairy's dime or quarter. As I watched her, I began to have an inkling of the concept and power of greed.

In the days preceding this event, she leaned over the edge of my crib many times and bared her teeth at me. She made unintelligible sounds while pointing to one of her incisors. She then grabbed it and began wiggling it just inches from my face. I tried to assume an expression of interest and sympathy, but what I really felt was bewilderment. Why would she do this? It seemed she was forcing the issue.

Finally, after days of this, came the big showdown. As I watched, and I am not making this up, she attached one end of a piece of string to the doorknob and the other end to her tooth. I saw what she meant to do. She pulled the door toward her, in readiness. She looked at me for support, and my heart went out to her. Her face, at that moment, was not the face of a mature, mercenary child. It was the face of a scared kid with a toothache.

She let the door slam and gave a shriek. She had been successful on the first try. Evidently, she had learned something from all those mailings. She picked up the tooth and rushed over to me. She was a sight. In her hand she held the tooth, which was interesting but not very attractive, and she smiled widely so that I could see the place it had come from. There was now a small gap between the other teeth with a little blood flowing from it. She was glowing with triumph.

Alerted by my sister's shriek, my parents joined us. They congratulated and comforted her. My father looked at me and raised his eyebrows as if to say, "Can you believe it?"

He then said, "This could happen to you."

I gave a start and shook my head.

When things settled down, my parents got me and my sister to bed. They tucked my sister in and assured her that the Tooth Fairy would come that night and take her tooth and leave her money. My sister, needless to say, was excited. She was to put the tooth under her pillow, and when she woke up, she would find what the Fairy had left.

When our parents were gone, she told me that she wanted to wait up for the Tooth Fairy and negotiate. I didn't think this was a good idea, but I was very curious about him. I decided that I would stay awake that night and although I wasn't about to help her negotiate,

I wanted to see what he looked like and discover how well he could bargain with my sister.

Despite her plan to wait up, my sister, exhausted by the ordeal of losing her tooth, was asleep in about three minutes. I stayed up. I waited and waited. The moon moved across the window. The house was silent. And dark.

I thought about my sister. She had been motivated by money and momentum and guided by her childlike maturity, yet what really stood out in my mind had been that moment of truth before she had slammed the door. She didn't have to do that. The tooth would have fallen out on its own, but she had wanted to be the boss in her own life and had, I saw now, bravely gone ahead. I thought she was great. I hoped he left her a dollar.

The clock ticked on. My eyes were getting heavy, but I felt that he would be here any minute. I tried to focus on the door of the bedroom. He probably had a lot of stops that night. I yawned again. The clock ticked on and on and, as I listened to it, time slowed down. The ticking became fainter and fainter. I strained to hear it. I took a deep breath and was fast asleep.

— From *Born with a Beard*

The Proposal

"Marry you? That's the sweetest thing anyone has ever said to me. Of course, I will."

My tears were frozen to my mustache and still she wanted to marry me!

Then we both heard it and looked to the sky. All the bells in town had begun to ring. I checked my watch — 2:26. What the heck? Tony Bennett started romantically humming. We both heard it.

"You sweetheart, how did you plan that?"

A flock of white doves wheeled overhead and sped off to the west. The stars came out.

"I, uh, ..."

A small gang of kids, bundled in parkas, passed us. They had these big, goofy grins and were singing softly, "Going to the chapel, and we're..."

Julie and I looked at each other. It was time for another kiss. More bells. More doves. A string quartet began Pachelbel's Canon. I hate that tune. I stopped the kissing.

"Let's try that again." We did. Mozart this time. Rose petals floated from out of the sky. There was applause. This was the greatest.

I said, "My mother will never believe it."

She said, "My big brother never liked you. But I'm sure he's over that. He'll think you're cute."

I gave her a look. She nodded. I liked him, too. But things had changed and she and I were together, at last.

I could see the headlines –

Gym Rat Benches Babe!
Love Conquers All!

I'd announce it in the gym newsletter —

Finally, Fit to Love!

I woke up the next day to pounding at the door. It was a big, beefy guy, with a mustache like the back end of a Zamboni.

"The name's Tony."

"You've got the wrong place, Mr...?"

"Tony, none of your business. No last name."

I laughed. "Are you for real, Mr. No Last Name?"

That's when he hit me.

He grunted, "What do you think?"

I got up off the floor. Blood was on the steps of my condo. I was hurting mad. Here's where my time at the gym was going to pay off.

Enraged, I said, "Look, Jack..."

"Tony."

"Whatever. What the hell is going on?"

Blood was flowing from my formerly perfect nose.

Zamboni answered, "You and Julie, fageddaboutit! I saw her first, so buzz off, punk!"

"You and Julie?! You're nuts! We're getting married. I proposed yesterday!"

He stared impassively.

"Give it up or she's a widow."

"Come on, man, get serious."

He hit me again.

"How about that? Serious enough for ya?" He turned and walked toward his car at the curb.

As I lifted my head, I saw the car. An over-sized sedan with black-tinted windows. The nearest glided down and a big paw gave me the finger. Love and fear began their struggle within me. Love was divine, but fear was really scary. Maybe I'd feel better after I cleaned up the blood.

I called Julie. "Do you know a guy named Tony?"

"Oh, no!"

"Oh, yeah. He just paid a visit to my nose with his fist. He's a monster!"

"I know. He's also a moron. I keep telling him to leave me alone and he says 'we're meant to be, we're family.'"

"That's weird. What's up?""

"He says it was arranged at birth."

"Huh?"

"Yeah, Dad said it must have been Mom. She's been dead for three years. She never told him."

"I know your name is Tortellini, but I never thought Sopranos. Not in Minnesota. It's too cold here. You're a blonde. Plus, we're too nice."

"Not Tony."

I couldn't argue. "What's his last name?"

"Fruili."

"For really?"

"No, you dope!"

"Ah, so it's drugs. That explains it."

"No! Fruili!"

"Wine?"

"Stop it! This isn't funny."

"You're right. My nose is killing me. Julie, do I need a gun?"

"Eddie! No!"

"I need to see you. Right now!"

"Okay. Come over, but use the back door."

"I'll do more than that." I hung up on her and got ready.

— From *Fit to Love, the endless Twitter Novel* (2009 – 2018)

There's a reason I'm here inside this book. It's the same reason you often find yourself beneath the covers where it's warm. For whether beneath or between, it feels safe. I haven't been out for a long time. I've been here waiting. Waiting for you. The two of us will keep each other company on this adventure. We'll help each other and take the other's hand when things get scary. We'll be each other's best friend and together we will see things and go places neither of us can now imagine. We will be together page after page and through the forest and on the water. Through the field and down the long winding road. Moving slowly between the clouds or hurrying across the road. It won't matter what happens or what the weather is like because we'll always end up between the covers safe and sound and glad we've had this time to get to know one another. Are you ready to go? Take my hand, the first part is a little rocky.

The Trojan Giraffe.

Eddie

Ted Ringer

The whole thing is an enigma
wrapped in a California roll.

Excerpts from The Books.

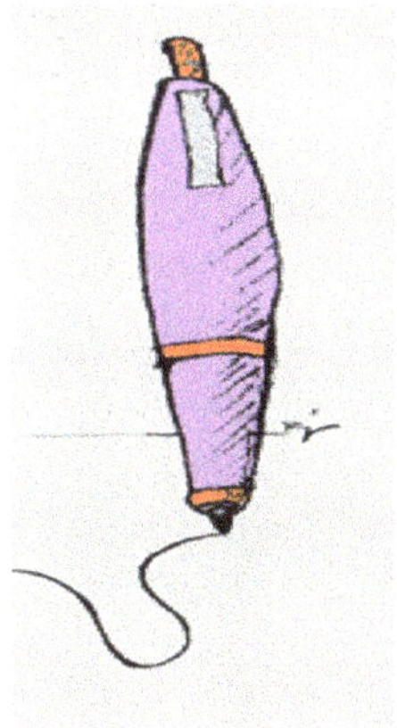

Reading

Reading is an infinite activity. Our government through its agent, The Library of Congress, insures this. The Library of Congress contains a copy of every book published in the United States. Books are everywhere and new ones are coming in all the time. The shelves are sagging with books of all sorts — from *He Doesn't Know I Care* to *A Modest History of the Universe.* Comic books to Encyclopedias. Books written by dedicated men and women of literature, compulsive egotists, celebrity Bar-B-Que masters, and people who didn't even realize they were writing a book.

Imagine how large this library must be. Curiosity trembles at the thought of this much information. Eyelids grow tired and breathing slows. The mind cannot encompass the existence of this many books. This is why we must read them one at a time.

It's an activity that can help put our feet on the ground while at the same time it takes us to places faraway. It expands our vision. If you live in Minnesota, reading can give you a sense of Texas or Tasmania. And if you live in Texas or Tasmania, you can learn the difference between Minneapolis and St. Paul and other fascinating things which you had no idea could make a difference. Outer Space is just pages away and you can come back any time you want. The past exists in the present and you can be a part of it. The opportunities are limitless.

Reading calms us down. Although it can be done, reading while walking or driving is not recommended. It is a reflective act. And reflecting at stoplights or on sharp curves can be dangerous. When we read, we are (most of us) sitting down. This in itself is beneficial. It keeps us from constantly doing errands. We leave behind the world, as we know it, and travel instantly to places we have never been and to places that may never have existed. This saves not only time but, also, airfare.

If you get lost, you can just go back a few pages and orient yourself. Unlike Television, which is anything but reflective, we can travel at our own pace and to wherever we want. On the way, we need not worry about hamburgers, or our cars, or whether we use the correct phone provider.

Reading is a cooperative act. As a reader, you and the author together, design new buildings, create hairdos, and resolve conflict. You can toy with affections, fly an airplane, and outwit the enemy. You can help bake a cake, bait a hook, or beat the system. It's endless. Just when things seem to be falling into that ditch called Routine, you can revive yourself with a new adventure, a new skill, a new direction.

So many books, so little time. So little time, so little time.

We Venture Outside

My sister let me know in many ways that, despite the fact that I was her brother, she considered me just a bit odd. This didn't bother me. I liked her. I looked up to her. How could I help it? She was twice my size. I figured I could learn from her mistakes. It seemed to me that parents, even my parents, had probably always been old but that my sister had once been young like myself and had been through many of the things I knew to be in my future. She had started school. She had lost some of her teeth. She had successfully negotiated a later bedtime. She was on her way. Hey, she could walk.

I loved and admired her, even though I hadn't told her so, and I would have done anything for her. So, when she came to me one day and said she wanted to show me something and that it was outside, I was very excited to see what it was.

Babies don't get to go outside much. We sleep a lot, we eat about every ten minutes, and everyone always wants to know how we are doing. All of that is great, but after a while you want a break. You want to go out and fill your baby lungs with some fresh air. Where I lived, the air, at this time of year, was about six degrees below zero. This sounds and is extreme, but I was unaware of what the implications of this might be. So was my sister.

I just wanted to do something different. She seemed to think it was important that I go with her, and I was ready. She bundled me up in an amazing array of sweaters and blankets. I looked less like a baby than I did Tuesday's load of wash, and I found it difficult to remain upright. My sister tied me and it all together with Mom's long scarf, stood back, and exclaimed, "Voila!" I could only roll my eyes and utter muffled baby sounds.

She topped it all off by putting Dad's joke hat on me. We called it that because he put it on when he told jokes. Poor Dad, although he was very funny, he knew only two formal jokes - the existential joke about the insurance salesman and the farmer and the one about the two, not so smart, football players from Iowa. Even at this early point in my life, I had heard these jokes many times. They were still funny and the hat always seemed to make them funnier. As I sat there, I kept falling over and my sister kept setting me back up. The hat was necessary, so that she could tell which part of me went where.

As we made our way out the door, my sister called, "We're going outside," to Mom, who answered absently from another room where she was involved in rearranging furniture. My sister carried me outside to the toboggan, which she had gotten for Christmas, and placed me on it, saying, "We'll take the shortcut."

She sat behind me with her legs on either side to keep me from falling off. She aimed us toward the swamp that lay at the bottom of the great hill that was our backyard and pushed. We were off.

The sun shone brightly as we hurtled down the hill. It was a beautiful day, and we began to travel through it at about thirty miles per hour. Snow flew into my face, and I began to laugh at the thrill of it. My sister was laughing, too. Over the sound of the wind in our ears, the rush of the snow, and the pounding of our childlike hearts we heard, quite faintly, something that sounded like our mother screaming.

We barreled forward. Together, we leaned to the right. The toboggan zipped past a tree that had threatened our progress. We threw our weight to the left, hit a little bump, and became airborne for a moment. My sister leaned forward and yelled "No brakes!" She was laughing hysterically. I'll never forget the excitement of that ride, the sense of freedom, the beauty of the winter all around us, and the feeling that nothing else existed or mattered except that moment and that hillside.

After what seemed like about two seconds, we reached the end of the hill and began to slow down. It was then that we knew for certain that it wasn't the wind, but that Mom really was screaming. Had she wanted to go with us, I wondered? I didn't have to wait long to find out.

Mom didn't have a toboggan, but she was at our side almost before we came to a stop. The first thing I noticed was that she didn't have her coat on. The next thing I knew, she was crying and hugging us. She was a little upset. I thought she seemed proud of the way we had handled the hill, but maybe I was reading into things.

She finally collected herself and sat back on her heels to look at us. Released from her hug and unsupported, I immediately rolled to one side. She propped me against my sister and sternly asked us what we thought we were doing.

I looked up at my sister for guidance and she said, "It was his idea."

Mom started laughing. At this, I smiled through the ice on my beard and knew that everything was going to be all right.

— From *Born with a Beard*

Go West

The year was 1872 and the word on the street was, "Go West, young man." This had first been uttered by a newspaperman back East, while in his cozy office. Minnesotans wondered about his remark. Though they knew that beyond where they lived was more land and space, they thought they were quite West already. At the edge of the frontier. And when they turned their faces into the wind and looked in that direction, what did they see? Not the Great Plains and Rocky Mountains of the West, but North Dakota. Or, if they looked a little lower, South Dakota.

They had heard the stories. One step over the border and those big spaces swallowed you up. The wind carried you away. Indians made off with your hair and left you lying staked out in the sun, slowly becoming a meal for the vultures circling overhead or for whatever wild animal came along. You'd consider yourself lucky if, anywhere in the midst of this nowhere, you came across another human being. And it would be a miracle if that human being were from Minnesota.

Minnesotans had gotten themselves as far west as Minnesota, and they thought it was a good place — plenty of room, more trees than you could shake a stick at, ten thousand lakes, a big river and weather. It wasn't the best weather. They noticed that the summers were hot and, in the evenings, the mosquitoes took over. They also noticed that the winters were a little long, but they had come as far as they were going, and they weren't going any farther. It was West to them.

— From *Gus Goes West*

Invention

Mid pleasures and palaces though we may roam
Be it ever so humble, there's no place like home

John Howard Payne

He stood at the end of a long line of inventors. This line consisted of himself, his father, and his father before him or, as we say in modern usage, his grandfather. This may not seem like a long line, but it involved over 100 years of trying to make something from nothing and, at the same time, keep food on the table. His father and grandfather had done just that and had done it with both style and success. Until he came along, the line had been quite straight, but not necessarily narrow.

His grandfather, Charles Maxwell Colvin, or Charles the First, as he liked to be called, had been a loud, overweight man with large whiskers. He had invented, among other things, a kind of tube that vastly improved radio reception. He always referred to this invention as "The Miracle." This one invention had made it possible for his family to live in luxury. It also allowed his grandson, the present inventor, to spend his childhood nights tuning in the important games from Chicago or rock and roll from Oklahoma City or news from Des Moines. His grandfather, had he lived, would probably have shuddered at the content of these programs, but it had been the device and its mechanics and not its ultimate uses that had sparked his interest.

The son of Charles the First, Charles Maxwell Colvin, Jr., had been called C.J. and hated to be referred to as Junior. He was a quieter man, perhaps subdued by his father's volume, and had, among his many creations, developed a sonar-based improvement during the war that the Navy snapped up and ordered into the classified mists. He was not enamored of the military, especially after this experience, and he spent the rest of his life working on items he thought might truly benefit mankind at large. Items such as comfortable hair curlers or a fountain pen that would write at any angle or, his favorite, a special nail polish for classical guitarists.

Both forebears had died while working. His grandfather, from a blow to the head, caused by a low beam of considerable thickness. He had encountered this as he responded to a bell, an invention of which he was quite proud, that signaled dinner. They found him on the floor of his workroom amidst half-finished projects. For once, he didn't look hungry. The father of our present-day inventor had died of an apparent heart attack possibly occasioned by a discovery no one could understand. His last words had been, "I think I've got it!" These deaths, in the line of duty, had a profound impact on Charles Maxwell Colvin III, known as Max. They scared him.

Max, the invention of his creative father and patient mother, had, without actually deciding such a course, steered himself away from inventing. As a student, he was receptive, though unfocused, and possessed enough curiosity to be considered dangerous by his teachers. Once out of school, he tried hard to place himself beyond the range of what his father had called, The Lure of the Garage — that being the place where all this inventing supposedly took place.

As a result, he had done ranch work in Wyoming. He had driven large trucks in Colorado. He had worked as a printer in Wisconsin. These had been wonderful experiences for him but, ultimately, they proved to be disasters.

In Wyoming, in response to what was referred to there as ornery critters, he created a system of metal fencing that caught on big time. In Colorado, at a desperate moment, he made a kind of tire chain out of plastic soda pop holders that, with a few modifications, went on to become standard equipment on mountain passes. And in Wisconsin, after he found himself threatening a printing press with a hammer, he came to his senses and devised a paper feeder which made the hammer unnecessary.

No matter what he did or where he went, it seemed he couldn't escape his heritage of inventing. It asserted itself at moments of crisis. It whispered to him as he showered in the morning. It suggested improvements as he crossed at the streetlight. It shouted at him as he balanced his checkbook.

He never intended to come up with these things. He had never worked in the methodical way of inventors to improve things; it never occurred to him. They simply popped out in response to a need and, as they did, Max feared that he was hearing that call of the garage he had been trying all his life to leave behind.

It worried him. He kept moving from place to place, but it did no good. He was afraid to lie down at night, because his dreams were filled with discoveries he would rather forget. A door knocker that tap-danced. A non-clogging drain. Unbreakable shoelaces. This kind of thing, this obsession with making, had killed his father and had indirectly brought about his grandfather's death and he wanted no part of it.

He tried hypnosis, he sought out non-materialistic religions, he considered the Foreign Legion but, in the end, he found that all driveways led to that innocent-looking hotbed of activity. The lure of the garage had proven itself too strong for him. His genes had spoken. His past had shaken hands with his present. He was going home.

— From *The Lure of the Garage*

THE READER

Hit the Road, Jack

The omens were dark. The vibrations bad. The diagnosis grim. The customers were angry and the employees irresponsible. Deliveries were uncertain and the cleaning crew had quit. The front window had been broken the night before by a big guy in a suit who mistook it for a door. The change was not adding up, and the partnership was feeling shaky. Minnie thought it might be time for a vacation.

Of course, it was always time for a vacation, but responsibility lay like a bad dream in his bones and he carried it around with him everywhere. It was just a job, wasn't it? But maybe it was more than that.

This bar had been his place of ungainly employment, his office, his stage, his throne for seven years. Not to mention the scene of long nights, painful diversions, and moments of bad judgement.

The other night a customer had said, with that special emphasis given to everything by an excess of alcohol, "Minnie, this place is like a big adventure every day."

Minnie, the boss, the man who knows, had turned to the drunken innocent and answered, "This is not an adventure, asshole, it's angina."

— From *Get Outta Town - A Tale of the Grateful Dead, the IRS, and Coffee*

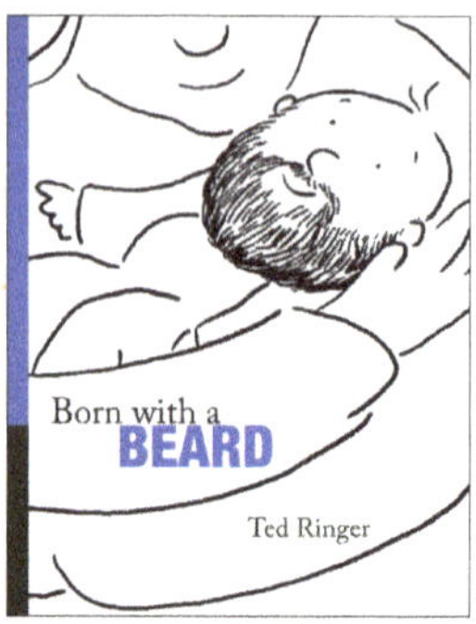

Mom Meets Dad

One day, my sister, who, for some reason, was interested in these things, asked Mom how she and Dad had met. It was afternoon, and we were lying around. Mom was reading, my sister was drawing, and I was staring out into space. We had a little time before dinner, so Mom, who at first blushed, smiled broadly and said, "Ok, here's the story."

"When I was a young woman, about twenty years old and at college, the great thing to do in the summer was to go to the beach. Everyone used to go. You wouldn't believe how many kids turned out. There were volleyball games in the sand, people were swimming and splashing around, some were tanning, some reading, and everyone was glad to be outside and near the water. There were groups of us girls who would sit together and talk about everything — politics, weather, each other, our figures — but we especially liked to talk about men. Or boys, as we called them.

"There were also groups of boys, though they probably thought of themselves as men, and they also were talking among themselves. It's hard for me to imagine what they were talking about, but, at that time, we hoped it might be about us. We didn't know anything about men. For all we knew, they were talking about their cars or of something unsavory or about philosophy.

"We all ate hot dogs and chips and soft drinks and talked and thought about the future out there under the sun. We sat around like this all day, every day. But at night, everything was different. The lights at the beach were dim and were swallowed up by the darkness and by the great expanse of water and sand. We built huge fires of driftwood. Half-lit by the fires or half-lit by the moon and the stars, the beach, with its soft sand and constant song of the waves, became a world of romance.

"The separate groups of girls and boys, who were shy by day, became a bolder, more friendly crowd by night. There were young fellows there with guitars, and we all sang together. We cooked more hot dogs. Boys and girls talked to each other, and some fell in love.

"I was interested in the boys, but I wasn't particularly interested in falling in love. I had school to think of, and there were many things I wanted to do. Plus, I had seen a lot of movies and had read quite a bit by this time and knew that there was a lot of heartache in the world.

"Well, one night I was standing by the campfire with my friend, Miriam, who was a nice girl and a gorgeous blonde to boot. We were singing the words to a popular song. I can't remember the name of it, but it was very sentimental. I looked across the fire and around at the circle of faces singing and I noticed a young man staring right at us. He was very bold. I thought, at first, that he was looking at Miriam. After all, she was the blonde. But no, he was looking at me. Before I looked away, I saw that he was tall and quite handsome, with dark hair. He was smiling.

"I looked up again and he was gone. I was so disappointed. I looked at Miriam to see if she had noticed, but she was still singing. The next thing I knew, someone tapped me on the shoulder. I turned and looked. No one was there. I felt a tap on my other shoulder. I turned and there was your father, the boy from the other side of the fire. He wasn't your father then. I had never seen him before. He was laughing and I told him that his little trick was stupid. He said, 'Yeah, I know.'

"Well, we got to talking, and it turned out that he was very nice. He had good manners and was really funny. It wasn't that he told jokes; he just had a sense of humor. He did tell one joke. He said it was an existential joke. It was the same one you've heard about the insurance salesman and the farmer, and I didn't think it was that funny, even then. But he was also serious and seemed very sweet. We talked about what we were studying at school, and he told me he was studying business.

"We went for a walk along the beach and talked for hours. When it was time for me to go home, he walked me back to where the crowd was and as we got closer, he began acting a little strange. He suddenly leaned over and kissed me. It was totally unannounced and unexpected, and I slapped him. I liked him, but it was a reflex. As soon as I slapped him, his face went white and he turned and threw up. It was the most amazing thing. At first, I thought it was because of all the hot dogs, but it turned out that he was in love with me.

"He was so embarrassed. I apologized and tried to reassure him that it was all right and that, in spite of what happened, I liked him, too. But he felt terrible. He gathered his dignity together and said that he was sorry he had kissed me. He said he realized that he had made a fool of himself. He looked me in the eye, said goodnight, and walked off.

"I went to find Miriam. She asked me where I had been, but I didn't know what to tell her. When I did tell her, she thought I was kidding. I discovered, by telling her about the whole thing, that even though he had thrown up, I really did like him.

"We went back to the beach every night. I looked for his face around the fire, but I never saw him. We sang the songs and had fun, but I kept looking for him. I wanted to tell him that everything was ok. I wanted to tell him something. Miriam thought I was crazy. One night, it was getting late and Miriam wanted to go home, but I persuaded her to stay for one more song. As I sang, I thought of how afraid we all are of each other and how big and lonely the world can be.

"I was looking at the fire, and I was thinking that it was almost the end of the summer, when I felt a tap on my shoulder. I turned and no one was there. I turned around the other way and there he was. He saw that I was glad to see him. He blushed and looked down at his feet and said, 'Hi.' "

My mother stopped then, and everything was quiet.

My sister and I looked at each other. We didn't know quite how to take this story.

My sister said weakly, "Wow."

I mumbled something and looked thoughtfully into the distance. Mom was smiling. She sighed, deeply, and got up to make dinner.

Dad Meets Mom

One afternoon we were all lying around the living room. All of us, except Mom. She was somewhere else. Out with The Girls or at the store. My sister, who I knew had been waiting for just the right moment, asked Dad how he had met Mom.

Dad was surprised. He blushed and said, "Oh, you know, we met, fell in love, and got married."

My sister said, "I know that, but how, where, when?"

Dad realized there was no way out of this and understood that he would never be able to return to his research on the couch, until he told her. He leaned back, looked at us, a receptive audience, and said, "Okay, here's the story."

"When I was a young man going to college back east, times were tough. The depression was on, and money was scarce. I studied business and was determined that when I got out of school, I would know how to make a living so that I could buy you two lots of presents. I was a serious young man and always had a job while I went to school. In the summers, I was a lifeguard at the beach.

"The beach was the big hangout, and all the kids were there each day. From my perch, in the chair, I could see thousands of young people up and down the beach. They were getting tan, playing, running, swimming, and talking. There were groups of guys talking about their cars and money and what they were going to do next week. There were also groups of girls who talked about whatever girls talked about — their mothers, fashion, sewing. Who knows? At night there were parties on the beach, but after a full day of lifeguarding, I was too tired for that. I always went back to my room, studied, and went to bed early.

"My job, as lifeguard, was to pay attention to what was happening out in the water, not on the beach. Most days, the most exciting thing that happened was that someone got sunburned and that was fine with me. I'd watch the people swimming, and I'd watch the waves roll in and I kept a lookout for sharks. That's right. Sharks. No one had actually seen one at this beach in eight years, but the possibility kept me on my toes.

"Every now and then, someone would swim too far out from shore, and I would race out there and help them in. Or someone's dog was a better swimmer than they were, but had a weak sense of direction, and

I'd go out and get them, too. Once in a while, something serious happened, a near drowning, and my fellow lifeguards and I would do everything we could to save someone. In the three years I worked there, no one died. Thank God. But we did have some close calls.

"One day, I was scanning the water and noticed someone out there, much farther than they should have been. This swimmer was way past the markers. I got up on my chair and attempted to wave him in. Of course, he didn't see me. He didn't look like he was in trouble, so I decided I would keep my eye on him until he came in and then I would go down and let him have it. This kind of thing was dangerous and really made me angry.

"As I watched this guy, I thought I saw something moving even farther out than he was. Maybe it was just a wave, but it made me nervous. Suddenly, my stomach turned over as I realized that it might be a shark. I used my binoculars and saw, to my horror, that this was much worse than any shark. This object moving toward the swimmer so quickly was a deadly, giant squid.

"I jumped from my chair, strapped my knife to my leg, and plunged into the water. I tore out away from the safety of shore. The water was freezing. I passed the markers in mere seconds and headed for the thrashing water ahead of me.

"When I got there, I found that the Squid had one long, creepy, tentacle wrapped around the body of the swimmer and held him, for a moment, high above the water. I was shocked to see that it wasn't a man, it was your mother. She wasn't your mother then. At that point, I had never even met her.

"The Squid saw me with its huge, bulging eyes. I shouted at it to let her go and pulled my knife and placed it between my teeth. I swam toward it. The Squid tossed your mother to one side and turned to face me. In the seconds before it attacked, I had the consoling thought that, at least, she was safe.

"Then there was no time for thinking. A slimy tentacle wrapped itself around my middle and pulled me to the oozing body of the Squid. If he could have, he would have thrown his head back and laughed. He was sure he had me in his power.

"I could hear your mother's screams, and I thought, whatever I do, I have to save her from this monster. I took my knife from my teeth and shouted to her to swim to shore. I barely got that out, before I was pulled, suddenly, beneath the water. Luckily, my arms were still free, and I began to attack the Squid with my knife. It was like going after a Grizzly with a toothpick, but it was all I had.

"I knew that if I could strike a sensitive place, the Squid might be stunned enough to release me. I stabbed repeatedly, but nothing happened. The noise was incredible. The water thrashed about me, and my heart pounded desperately. My breath was almost gone but worry would do me no good. I could only keep stabbing the Squid and hope that I would get lucky. Time slowed, and our struggle seemed to go on forever. Things started to look pretty bleak. My strength began to desert me.

"Suddenly I was being lifted from the water. I looked down and saw the black cavern of the Squid's giant jaws waiting for me. I knew I had only one chance, and I threw my knife with every ounce of strength that remained. It went straight into the cold, cruel eye of the beast and there was a terrible sound — part thunder and part cry of agony.

"The next thing I knew, I was flying through the air and hit the water on my back with a force that knocked the wind out of me. A wave of panic shot through me, and then everything went black. Seconds later, I regained consciousness and realized that your mother was with me and that she was holding my head above water. Our battle was over. We were both safe. As we looked out to sea, we saw the mass that had been the Squid sink slowly into the icy depths. Your mother and I then helped each other back to shore and, as they say, the rest is history."

My sister and I, as you can imagine, were on the edge of our seats and breathless after this story. It was so amazing.

After a few moments my sister managed to say, "But Mom told us a story about how you met that was completely different."

My father simply looked at her and said, "Well, you know how it is, women are such romantics."

— From *Born with a Beard*

Meanwhile…

Minnie hadn't sat down since the show had started. He had his air guitar going. The girls were dancing in an innocent yet completely sensual way that warmed his heart.

Krazy Kat peeking through a lace bandana
Like a one-eyed Cheshire
Like a diamond-eyed Jack

Minnie's burly self was moving in its own world. The band was cooking. Minnie, by definition, was taking up space. His dancing had escalated along with the music and those in the seats next to him gave way to his effort and to his controlled recklessness. Carried away, he turned it on and turned it loose. His eyes were closed and he shook and he shimmied, while his feet described the indescribable. His entire body became suggestive and ecstatic. Time stood still, but the dance continued.

The band moved flawlessly into *I Know You Rider* and to anyone who turned to watch him, it wasn't really Minnie they saw. He had become something else, bigger than just a big guy dancing. He had become love, sex, music, breath, movement and there it was, right in front of them, exulting in itself and in the fact that all of them were there together.

As the song came to an end, Minnie dipped once more and, in perfect time to the music, he reached upward and shot out of his body. He didn't need wings to propel him. The air became thinner, the stars popped out of the sky, which had turned a deeper blue, and, for a moment, everything was still. Then, slowly, he floated back down to Earth and to Susan and to those around him, who could only applaud and smile in wide admiration.

Meanwhile, the band played on.

— From *Get Outta Town – A Tale of the Grateful Dead, the IRS, and Coffee*

Singing His Song

Gus Johnson didn't think about the West or North and South Dakota or anywhere else. He was a busy guy and he had a job. What he thought about mostly, were girls, beer, music, and some of the more tender emotions. His job included all of these, and in this, he considered himself lucky. He was a musician and singer in a polka band called "Oscar and the Blue Gills." They were a popular band and, though Minnesotans were a hard-working bunch and should have been in bed, it seemed that the band was playing somewhere most nights of the week.

The Blue Gills oompahed their way up and down Hennepin Avenue in Minneapolis, and in and out of doors on 7th Street in St. Paul. They played train depots in little towns on the prairie, where families danced and raised dust, and they played saloons deep in the woods, where they were surrounded by tall men with beards, carrying axes. They played grand houses out at the lake, where the boys were on their best behavior and hardly anyone fell down.

Life for Gus was one party after another and that made what was to come all the more upsetting. He thrived on this life. He sang. He shouted. He put beer away with the best of them. He winked at the girls, who blushed and turned away and then shyly looked back, and he winked at their mothers, who did the same. When he sang the words:

Oh, my beautiful one
How can you leave me?

he meant them and sometimes he got so worked up that the song would end with Gus looking at the floor, just sighing the words, with tears on his cheeks. Oscar Olson, who was older and played the banjo, would lean over and put his arm around Gus and nod at the applauding crowd, as if they were all family.

Gus had a good, clear voice. He could belt out a drinking song, of which there were many, in a voice that could, and had, tapped kegs. He could sweetly warble a love song in such a way that each woman listening suddenly found herself alone, in soft focus, thinking of her sweetheart. And if she didn't have one, thinking of Gus.

Between the drinking and the girls and the music, Gus felt that no one could be as fortunate as he. He liked the life he led and tried to put his feelings into words and music. He was nineteen years old and he had written his first song.

It was called, "My Sweet Flower." The lyrics went like this:

Growing in your garden
Where you once were sown
Feeding on the sunshine
Soft and all alone

By breezes drifting softly
I catch a whiff of you
My heart pounds like the tuba
Oom pah oom pah doo

Soon we will be married
I wonder what we'll do
My heart sounds like a tuba
Oom pah oom pah doo

It was his first song. Don't judge it too harshly.

There would be others.

Besides singing, he could play a mean accordion. His fingers flew over the buttons and keys and, when he pumped the box, he put his whole body into it. His eyes were closed in rapture on the ballads, and on other songs, they rolled wildly as he sang, arms pumping:

I don't want her
You can have her
She's too fat for me

He also played guitar and harmonica, though not as well or as naturally, so he practiced all the time. This both delighted and annoyed his neighbors. In the beginning, it had delighted them and then, when they realized that he might never stop, it began to annoy them.

The future that spread out before him was always soft in the darkness of the evening and shaded by clouds of foam. It never occurred to him that things could change. He pictured himself growing old, playing in the band like Oscar, and winking his way through life and romance. He was confident that his world would spin in three-quarter time and any sad times would quickly be replaced by an upbeat, happy song and a cold glass of beer.

Gus looked in the mirror and saw a tall, handsome young man, whose eyes were green, whose dark hair parted on the right, and whose ears were unobtrusive. His long arms hung at his side, and he tilted his head and wiggled his eyebrows at himself in a way he thought might be debonair.

As he examined himself, he thought, I'm young, I'm good-looking, and I can dance. This was as deep as his philosophy went. He smiled widely at his reflection. He glanced out the window and saw the great Mississippi rolling by and thought, 'What exciting thing is going to happen next?' He thought, 'I'm a Minnesotan and I like it here.' He thought, 'What was her name?' and began to scratch his head.

There was a lot to think about. Things were good and the thought, which never entered his mind, was the one which said, 'Go West, young man.' As far as he knew, he was here to stay.

— From *Gus Goes West*

May Day!

"We're going down!" Max shouted above the noise.

He could see the flames from the number two and four engines. Smoke was coming into the cockpit and he saw the navigator slumped over in the corner. He turned to his co-pilot.

"Smitty, go back and check on Rawlins and prepare to bail out." Max cupped his mask to his mouth and screamed, "Mayday, Mayday," and gave out their coordinates. The smoke was getting thick and he had all but lost control of the plane. They were over enemy territory and Max had been hit in the leg. He could feel the warm blood as it ran into his boot.

He heard a voice call his name. He turned and saw his father standing there in his lab coat. "May I talk with you for a minute?"

"Dad, we're going down!" Max couldn't believe this.

"Just for a second," his father said, in a calm voice that was compelling. Max undid his shoulder harness and walked toward the back of the plane.

Suddenly, everything was quiet and they were sitting at one of the workbenches in the garage.

Max took a few deep breaths and the adrenaline receded somewhat. He was still quite jumpy. His words stumbled out. "That was close. You showed up just in time. Another minute and we were goners."

"Goners?"

"That's the way we talk in the service. I'm glad to see you." And Max, flush with battle and with a new lease on life, got up and hugged his father. They were both awkward, not having had much practice at this in real life.

Despite not being able to give himself entirely over to the embrace, Max's father was touched and, for once, without words.

"I had almost given up hope that you'd come back," said Max.

His father replied, "I don't really know how this dream stuff works but I felt I had to see you again. To help with the work and... and just to be here."

Max filled his father in on his progress and had his guess confirmed that C.J. had been working on a way to prolong life. When he told him about the microscope and that he was using samples from his own body, his father grimaced and said that wasn't very scientific, but that he had done the same thing.

C.J. explained that he had been looking for a way to manipulate the cells of the body to prevent disease and the general weakening that occurred with age. He had been searching for a compound he was convinced could be found in Nature, that would somehow bolster the body's recuperative and restorative powers, far beyond what they normally were. He said that if he could only discover this and apply it, life, as we know it, might be lengthened by many years.

"What about the *Hokey Pokey*?" Max asked.

"This might sound crazy, but I have a feeling that music is going to turn out to play an important part in this. I had studied a lot about Tracheophyta and photosynthesis and..."

"Wait a minute. What? Tracheo what?"

"Vascular plants. Land plants, ferns, seed plants. Trees, shrubs, broccoli. Anyway, there is extensive literature that describes how these plants respond to music. A kind of audio synthesis. And the more I researched this, the more I became convinced that music might be an important element in the whole process. You know, it's like those ads for sun lamps and how 30 minutes a day can cure the winter depression a lot of people feel. It's a lack of sunlight. I believe a similar thing occurs because of a lack of music."

"Any music?"

"Well, so far, all I know is that game show theme songs don't seem to have any effect. I'm not sure what the ideal music is, but I'd say it should be something snappy. Maybe something like Burl Ives or Al Hirt."

Max looked at his father. He had implicit faith in his abilities, but he knew Burl Ives was not snappy.

"What else?"

"Well, there isn't much else. My theory is that a combination of a daily dose of the right substance, a kind of vitamin, if you will, and the right kind of music will somehow strengthen the cells and recharge their batteries."

"How am I going to find this vitamin?"

"Experiment. It's the only way."

Max felt that he now had a couple more pieces to the puzzle, but he still had a lot of questions.

Before he had a chance to ask, his father said, "Max, I wished we could have worked together when I was alive. You're the son I've always wanted."

Max forgot his questions and gently told his father, "I'm the son you always had."

C.J. looked away. "Maybe we're making up for lost time."

They faced each other and, after a moment, they embraced. Max closed his eyes and silently forgave his father for everything.

He opened his eyes and, suddenly, he had a sinking feeling in his stomach. His leg was killing him and Smitty was hovering over him.

"Captain! Rawlins is gone. Bailed out already. He left this note."

Max took the note, though his hands were shaking violently with the erratic motion of the plane. Through the smoke that was beginning to choke him, he was barely able to make out the words on the paper.

Max smiled and looked up from the note. He saw the familiar pictures on the wall and felt the marshmallow that was his bed, beneath him. His leg was asleep and his neck hurt, but the war was over. He had made it back in one piece.

— From *The Lure of the Garage*

A Couple More Songs

A couple more songs and Jerry and Bobby and the others laid down their instruments and left the stage to the two drummers, who took most of the crowd with them to a place where time was skewed and space expanded, the drums talking to each other and the crowd dancing.

After almost twenty minutes of pounding, noodling rhythm, the band returned and joined them in outer space. The guitars wailed in an eerie way, melody stumbled in one direction and then another and then, finally, miraculously, it all began to coalesce. The bass got in step with the notes of the guitars. The drums fell in behind them and suddenly the band was into the first bars of *The Other One* and they were off.

The afternoon continued and, mercifully, the clouds came up to cut the heat and throw a little shade on the audience. They needed it, because the band would not let up. The light had changed into that soft, late afternoon glow and Minnie wondered how long the band could continue. When they broke into *One More Saturday Night,* he knew that this would be the last song. It built and built, driving everyone crazy. Jerry threw out licks no one could believe, Phil's bass thumped, and Weir sang the words celebrating this and all Saturday nights in the past and in the future.

With one last refrain and the final chomp, chomp, chomp of the guitars, it was over and the crowd erupted with a roar.

— From *Get Outta Town – A Tale of the Grateful Dead, the IRS, and Coffee*

Fit to Love — Campaign Edition

I was determined to live in the world I wanted to live in and not be dissuaded by a reality I would never understand. Was I that different from most people? It was the wanting and the trying, the safari of effort that was important. Not that I was on safari. I was a seeker, not a hunter. I had a vision, not an appetite.

James Brown had given me the confidence to push forward through the jumble of human relations and reach my goal. Or keep dancing until my shoes wore out. I'd stop being such an introvert. I would become a man of the people. Hell, I'd run for office!

That's the ticket! so to speak. Involvement, participation, service to others, dedication to principles, and a bunch of other stuff. I'd stand up for the disenfranchised and unloved. I'd fight for the right of anyone to be loved and to fall in love. No matter what age.

I went out the door, with a wide smile on my face, and entered the nearest bar. I ordered a Budweiser and looked the bartender in the eye. I stuck my hand out to introduce myself. He looked at me, assessing an obviously new contender. "Dude, that's five bucks." I hadn't yet declared my candidacy, so I wasn't hurt, but I did think that was a little steep and said so.

"Times are tough all over. I'm just trying to make a living." This was good info. A small business owner. The man in the street. Well, bar.

I asked him how he felt about love. Eyes narrowed, he wished me good luck and walked away to confer with one of my future constituents.

As I said, I saw this as all good information. I pictured myself as the Love candidate. Although, in these times, maybe that wasn't enough. I'd broaden my appeal. I could enlist the young. I still considered myself part of that gang. They/we were all optimists.

I'd speak to service organizations, at lunch meetings. Lunch was always a favorite time for me. The possibilities were endless. What a menu! Optimists. See? Elks, Rotarians, Rastafarians, Masons, Odd Fellows, Sons of Knute, Daughters of the Revolution, Kiwanis, Lions, Shriners. The Sons of the Desert. Foresters, Hibernians, Native Sons of the Golden West, The Royal Antediluvian Order of Buffaloes. I mean endless — Chambers of Commerce, Knights of Columbus, Mooses, Owls, Orioles, Lutherans.

I'd rally the troops at Home Depot. "My fellow Suburbians, our list is long, our supplies plentiful, our tools innumerable. Let's do this!"

I'd avoid Wal-Mart, but I was aiming at Target. "My fellow Shoppers, Love is where you find it and I've found it everywhere! In Home Furnishings, there is comfort, warmth, and a certain design je nais se quoi. I've recharged my batteries in Electronics. In Boys, I've gotten in touch with my inner child. We all know Automotive, so I won't go there, but School Supplies is a real education. My platform of Love is an important one. Stop by Greeting Cards on your way out and help me spread the word. We each have a flame of hope, a spark of desire, a dream of love within us. Join me at Checkout and vote with your wallets."

I went out to meet the people and appealed directly to them to forward our Love agenda. This was a political revolution of Love. It might be an independent movement, but it took two to tango. It required all of us to get together and declare our intentions. We needed to pledge our love, plight our trough. I mean troth. (That kind of self-serving is so old school), and shout our love to the electorate.

I made the rounds of the fast-food parlors. What better way to a voter's heart, than through his or her stomach? I told them... "It's the special Love sauce that holds our party together. Bring a friend to the booth this November and satisfy that patriotic hunger." I hit the grocery stores and set up a little table between organic vegetables and donuts, demonstrating our broad appeal and diversity.

I ventured out into the August heat and greeted voters on the street, at the swimming pools, and in the parks. While I was there, I fed the pigeons and the squirrels and tried out my new slogans. "Shake a tail feather and vote!" "Endorsed by Rocky. And Bullwinkle!" "Nuts? Get to know me!" Even the geese were interested, though they were Canadians.

I went to get my hair trimmed. "Politics is just as important as good grooming, it's about style, but it's what's inside that counts." I attended the Farmer's Market. "Fair Trade is a sign of a healthy relationship. Let's plant the seeds for a great harvest in November!" At the County Fair, there were voters who only ventured from the farm a couple of times a year. I felt honored to make their acquaintance. They might have stayed on the fence, but I knew a thing or two about critters and, eventually, won their trust.

I went to the dog park and made the rounds, shaking hands, patting backs, and growled my message to everyone I met. As I told them, "We form a tribe, a country, a people!" A few heads turned up at me. "A people with wonderful dogs!" Tails wagged. "Find your voice, shout your message, unleash your essence!" They howled. They were now part of a movement. Moved by powerful emotions. As one, though somewhat undisciplined, they headed for the exits, determined to take the message back to their respective neighborhoods.

I stood there stunned. By what had just happened and by what had been happening. Was I the same guy? The lost introvert? The lonely boy? Holy cow! I could get used to this. I liked the new me. I felt, for the first time, that I might actually help someone. At last, I had a purpose besides the seemingly quixotic search for personal love. I wanted everyone to have an equal chance at it.

Not that theirs would be quixotic. Theirs might be aquatic, for all I knew. I just wanted to change the conversation. I wanted to adjust the focus from one of greed, illusion, and war to one of love, possibility, and hope. I'd give voice to everyone's dream.

That sounds ambitious, I know. But it seemed like a message people were ready to hear. To me, it seemed timely and essential. Sure, some have laughed and called me naïve, but others said, What the hell? I can't help but be encouraged. It is going to be an uphill battle, pardon the warlike metaphor, but I will never concede. I will stay true to my campaign of true love.

I'll never lose my idealism and vision, as others have before me, and get carried away by ego and a big infusion of money. I probably don't have to worry about money. Where I come from love has always been something that was given away.

Sure, it would be great to win, but after these last few weeks on the road, I've become a realist... The kind of realist who doesn't care anymore about winning or losing. I've become the kind that just wants to stay real. I want to remain true to my beliefs, my principles, my desires (if I may say so), no matter what obstacles or temptations turn up. Win or lose, I am steadfast in my desire (that word again) for a better world, a better country, an America that knows its own heart. It's lonely out there, on the campaign trail, but I've asked my key aides to alert me, if I ever use the word desire again.

Running for office should be a selfless act, even if, like everyone else, I yearn for love. Isn't that what it's all about? Each American has certain unalienable rights such as life, liberty, love, and the pursuit of happiness. I want to protect these rights. I'll continue to speak out, no matter the opposition. The other candidates never get bogged down in details and neither will I.

I'm the only serious candidate without questionable incidents in his or her past. Perhaps, in comparison, mine just seem trivial. My position on the issues remains steady, though the others may waffle, distort, temporize, evade, and, sometimes, make false statements. I never lose my cool. I was never that cool to begin with. I'm slow and steady and I hope to win the race. Or at least, make a difference.

I'm having my own debate. Come on down to the West End Tavern. I'll ask myself the hard questions and I'll always tell you the truth. Even when that truth is inconvenient. Yes, at one time, I broke someone's heart. I didn't mean to, but, sometimes, you can't avoid it. Given the choice of right versus wrong, hard work versus expediency, love or hate, I know you are familiar with my record.

I'm concerned for our future. Heck, I'm concerned for my future. I want what so many of us want — love and a job. New revelations about the candidates occur every day, but what you learn about me will never shock you, though you may scratch your head. We can talk about what's really important: understanding one another, tolerance for boneheads, and love for whoever suits you.

This election is more important than you know. Casting your vote will not only change the direction of things but will make you feel good. You will feel part of the electorate. One of the people who care about this great country and its complicated love life. Keep the faith, tell your friends and neighbors. Spread the word to complete strangers. Include them. And in November, turn up, turn on, and vote what your heart wants you to.

Listening To Music

One day I was relaxing in my crib, reading. I heard my father singing, down in the den. Although he loved music, it was rare to actually hear him sing anything. The words drifted up to me...

In my adobe hacienda
There's a touch of Mexico
Cactus much lovelier than orchids
Blooming in the patio

I was fascinated. As he sang, the melody took me to another place. A place near the desert where the light was always changing and where there wasn't any snow. I knew instinctively that this was another kind of romance and I wanted to be part of it. I closed my eyes and saw myself riding toward an impossibly distant horizon, my beard flowing in the breeze.

I was not riding aimlessly through the great West. I had a destination. I was headed for Rosa's Cantina, where there was a girl I knew. Granted, not a very nice girl, but she was beautiful, and to dance with her was as close to heaven as this cowboy could imagine. Plus, the food at Rosa's was great - hot dogs, fries, and shakes. No baby food there and the bottles they served weren't warm. They were cold and full of sugar.

I tied my pony to the rail outside and made my stiff-legged way through the swinging doors. It was quite a lively crowd for a school night. In the corners were poker games that looked like they had been going on for some time. The bar was full, and an unhealthy-looking guy was playing the piano, while a few couples danced. I bellied up to the bar and looked around.

The bartender came over and said, "Nice beard. What'll it be?"

I looked at him closely to see if he was mocking me. He wasn't. "Vanilla shake," I said, "and hurry it up. I've been in the saddle all day."

He returned with the shake, and I downed half of it in one gulp. It had been a while since I had had one and I immediately got one of those pains in my forehead. I didn't want anyone to think I was a greenhorn, so I stood there in motionless agony with a look I hoped might pass for a smile.

From beside me a sweet, dark voice said, "Hey stranger, you don't look so good."

I gasped and said, "Don't bother me. I'm thinking."

I opened my eyes and saw her there, that wicked Felina, the girl that I loved.

She smiled at me, said, "See you later," and walked out into the crowd and up to the biggest, meanest guy I had ever seen. They began to dance.

I don't know if it was love or the shake or the long ride or what, but I saw red. I knew she didn't love me and probably didn't love anyone, but I wasn't going to let her dance with that brute. I went up to them, in the middle of the dance floor, and cut in.

The big guy stood there for a moment fuming and then grabbed me and lifted me off the floor, with a loud, frightening growl.

Everyone stopped and looked at us. The piano was silent. The only sounds were my spurs turning slowly, three feet off the ground.

"Why don't you go back to your Mama?" he snarled. "Of course, she probably thought you were a dog, not her baby boy."

He turned to the crowd and laughed.

His breath was terrible. My beard quivered.

I passed over the remark about my mother and said, "You must have said Roy, not boy. No one calls me boy."

I gave him the worst look I had. It wasn't bad enough.

He carried me outside to my pony, put me in the saddle, and said, "Git. And don't come back until you're old enough."

"Old enough for what?" I asked, defiant to the end.

I glanced at Felina, in the doorway, and through her giggles she waved sweetly to me. I made a silent vow to return.

At that instant, the big galoot smacked the back of the pony with his six-shooter, and I was on my way into the night.

A little way down the trail, my pony stumbled badly, and it jolted me out of my disappointment and shame. I noticed that it was light out and a song was running through my head.

When setting sun says the long day is done
Sweet music starts to fill the air
In my adobe hacienda,
Life and Love are everywhere

I raised my head and there was my father looking down at me. He was smiling and he said, "Well, old timer, how about a bottle?"

— From *Born with a Beard*

Aachoo!

One day, Gus woke up early. Well, what was early for him. Actually, it was late in the morning, but that's normal for a musician. His early was most people's late and his late could barely be imagined by the average citizen. He and everyone else met somewhere in the middle, went a few rounds, and then parted ways. While most sensible people were in bed dreaming, Gus was stomping on the bandstand or jamming with other hot accordion players in a smoky back room.

This morning, he woke up with a sneeze. It wasn't pleasant. He looked out the window and saw by the faint light that it was way too early for him. He rolled in the tangled sheets and arranged his hands beneath the pillow. He breathed deeply. He might have fallen back into unconsciousness but, just at that moment, he sneezed again and the force of it scattered all possibility of sleep. He sneezed once more, as if to confirm the situation.

He sat up in bed and put his hand to his head, checking for fever. Having established his apparent health, he became distracted by his stomach. He realized that breakfast, somewhere, was waiting and he swung his feet to the floor. In his life, food was a necessity.

That night, on the bandstand, he found that his eyes were watering and not from his being carried away by the lyrics and music. They itched, too. He was sniffling and, yet, he didn't have a cold. He had always been healthy. "Too young to be sick," his mother always told him.

He blinked all of it away as the band plowed through the list of songs for the night; although it seemed that, as the evening went on, his voice was changing, getting a little lower, a bit huskier. During

"She's the Girl Who Does the Laundry," Oscar gave him an inquiring look, but Gus just shrugged, not really understanding what was wrong either.

The next night was the same, only worse. Gus had to clear his throat repeatedly and he had a handkerchief in his back pocket for his sniffles. Oscar talked with him before the show and Gus told him he wasn't sick, just afflicted, and Oscar said that he hoped he wasn't allergic to beer. They both laughed at the thought.

As the night progressed, his symptoms grew worse. His eyes watered, his voice cracked, and he was forced to resort to his handkerchief often. Gus was disturbed and embarrassed, but the crowd thought he was being transported by emotion and clapped all the louder. The worse he felt, the more inspired the crowd thought he was.

He was singing *"Your Mama Knows I Love You"* which had a tricky accordion part and it was all he could do, during the solo, to keep his hands on the keys and not let the song fall apart by rubbing his eyes. As it was, he was so distracted that he sang the refrain four times in a row.

No matter how hard I try
You won't believe me
But you know who does
It's your Mama

It threw the band off, but no one else noticed.

The last straw came in the third set. Gus had had two beers during the break, with medicinal intent, and had another with him on the stand. Before starting, he concentrated all his effort on banishing these symptoms, which had now moved beyond annoyance and had begun to seriously affect his performance. He breathed deeply. He closed his eyes. He took another drink. To his surprise, this seemed to work for the first two or three songs.

There were no sniffles, no itching watery eyes. His voice had rejoined its accustomed pitch and his playing was unconscious. Oscar looked relieved and the whole band moved into each succeeding song with hope and abandon. Gus sent a prayer of thanks somewhere and launched into *"Our Love is Like an Apple."* He was at the end of the second verse when it happened.

She wondered and she asked me
If I could be believed
And so I tried to show her
She said she'd been ....

It was near the end of that last line, where the melody lifts itself up to a new height before gliding into the chorus, that the sneezing started. The entire audience jumped at the explosion and the band did, too. After a few startled and ragged notes, the band played on bravely, but Gus was still sneezing.

The people on the dance floor stopped in mid-step and all turned toward the stage to witness an attack of sneezing, such as few had ever seen. The song fell apart as Gus was almost lifted off the stage by the force of each outburst. His accordion hung heavily from his shoulders and was set swinging, with a little honking noise, at each new sneeze.

Finally, Oscar took control of the situation and led Gus off stage. There was a moment of silence, if you could call it that, with Gus sneezing continually, and then the band, what was left of it, began to play *"The Too Tight Polka."* Their hearts just weren't in it and the crowd began to thin out pretty quickly.

Gus eventually was able to take a break from his attack. Seated at a table, he apologized to Oscar and the other Blue Gills. They waved his apologies away with real concern for their friend and colleague. Diagnoses were made: too many burgers, too many late hours, too much beer. A musician's life is one of excess and everyone in the band was well aware of this.

The tuba player suggested too much kissing and heads turned toward him in derision. The sneezing resumed. The speculation continued.

When he was finally able, Gus brought all this to a halt by declaring that he had decided to see a doctor. They gasped. Medicine, at that time, was considered, at best, an inexact science and was treated as a last and desperate resort.

To his astonished friends, Gus said, "I'm young, I'm good-looking, and I can dance."

All heads nodded in assent.

"But this sneezing is getting in my way. I appreciate your concern, but none of these explanations feel right. The Doc will know."

The sneezing began again and did seem debilitating. The boys in the band looked at each other, their faces full of concern.

Over the noise, one of them said, “It’s your funeral.”

— From *Gus Goes West*

Good Form

The band was in good form and when Jerry went into a solo and it really began to take off, the rock-and-roll energy of it could be felt by everyone. Thousands of arms waved in the air. The crowd reacted with their own wild sounds and wordless exclamation, answering the series of notes that Jerry was playing.

Each note seemed to rearrange their DNA. The music was loud. It was one of those days where everything was working together. People danced with each other. They danced with themselves. They sang along. It got better and better. Twirlers twirled, joints were passed, and the tunes rolled on. All through the crowd, people turned to each other to make sure they weren't dreaming and to confirm the fact that the unbelievable thing they had just heard had really happened.

At moments throughout the afternoon, there was an overwhelming poignancy when Jerry sang certain lyrics like "I will survive" or "When I'm gone" or "I'll stay with you." Everyone knew he had been in a coma and had almost died.

The band had been together for thirty years and they knew that nothing lasted forever — not Jerry, not the band, not themselves, not this moment — and it made it all the more urgent and powerful. When Jerry sang these words, the crowd felt it and sent him a love that was undisguised and immediate. He responded with the music. They loved him and he loved them and this love expanded outward from all of them. These were the words and the feelings that had kept the scene alive for so long.

— From *Get Outta Town - A Tale of the Grateful Dead, the IRS, and Coffee*

Traffic Had Stopped

Traffic had stopped. A guy was about to get into a cab, but neither he nor the cab was moving. Was he frozen in the same moment as we were? Nothing moved. It was silent. As I gazed at her, I wondered exactly who this girl was. I mean, woman. She was a lot more powerful than I had thought. And more wonderful. She was smiling. She was twinkling. Was this love? Or something much weirder? Once we turned the corner, everything came back to life. As if it had never happened.

I asked, "Where to now?"

Was I a trusting soul or an idiot? Hmm... She turned to me.

"Eddie, we're on a mission."

I blanched and said, "Blanche, that may be more of a commitment than I'm ready for." I began to wonder what I had gotten myself into.

I asked again, "Where to?"

Her smile grew wider. "My place." She said it like it was a kind of exclusive club. I hoped it was.

She had a garden-level apartment, but the only garden was a pot outside the door with a withered stalk in it. There were bars on the windows. Does that sound creepy? Well, it wasn't. I mean, it looked creepy, but once inside I forgot all about it.

She told me to make myself at home, while she changed into, "something more comfortable to slip out of."

She had an aquarium with no fish, a blank globe, a bookshelf with only one book, and a sink full of dishes. You're probably wondering what that one book was. I looked and found that it was, **The Joy of Cooking.** She mentioned later that all of life was contained within those covers.

For all my need for love, I wasn't one of those guys who can just fall into bed with anyone they meet. Or was I?

As I waited, I looked at the aquarium. I realized my mouth was dry, my hands were shaking, and my knees had begun to sweat.

She was taking a long time. Except for the aquarium, it was quiet. I thought I heard voices, but it could have been the TV next door. I continued waiting. I had been there so long, I almost checked the fridge. I restrained myself, although I did eat some Cheetos that were on the counter.

Idly, I began checking out the envelopes on her desk. I looked up and found her staring at me. Embarrassed, I stammered, "I, I got bored."

She batted her incredible lashes. "Come here. I'll fix that."

Waves of heat came off her in waves. I'm not kidding. Her lips were like two cherries, ripe for the picking. Her skin was like satin. She was a goddess. Well, like a goddess. I was thinking like a bad novel. My shirt hung open to my navel. Was my neck breaking out because of the gold chain?

That part about the shirt and the gold chain isn't true. In fact, no words formed in my mind at all. I just stood there. I couldn't move. I was afraid my immobility had ruined her entrance. She slowly looked me up and down. I didn't know if it was for her benefit or mine. She floated to where I was rooted.

She was brief and to the point. "Kiss me."

This broke the spell or cast it or something.

It was a night too feverish to remember and too sensational to forget. The next morning, I woke, still flushed. She was not beside me.

I croaked, "Loosey? It's me, Ricky!"

It turned out I was there all alone. I found her note on the counter. It read, ***Duty calls. I'll be gone for two years. Lock the door behind you. You're not my type.***

What about our love? Or, at least, last night? Was I nothing but a plaything? (I love that kind of talk.)

Dismissed and humiliated, I promised never again! Next time, I'll know better. Once again, I had tossed everything out the window for a chance on love. But no such luck. Was my heart destined for extinction or excitement?

I determined to put my focus elsewhere. Like, Cleveland. Or rodeo. Or anything that had to do with boats. Or something.

First, I needed to plan. I needed to think. I wasn't good at either, but I had to try. I had gotten some sleep, though I had been mostly an accomplice to her exciting insomnia.

— From *Fit to Love - an endless Twitter novel.*

It Ain't Good

He told himself, "I need a real doctor."

His knock was mysteriously anticipated, and he heard a gruff voice bark, "Come in, it's getting late."

This sounded ominous. He sneezed loudly, gathered his courage, and entered.

Dr. Pedersen was sitting behind his desk, intently trimming his fingernails. Without looking up, he snapped, "Take a seat."

The large room was silent, except for Gus's sniffling and the thin snipping of fingernails. Gus examined the doctor and, because he was nervous, became a little irritable and decided that this doctor didn't look good. The top of his head looked old and his white hair hadn't been combed. He hadn't shaved recently and Gus wondered why he wasn't paying attention to his patient. Gus sniffled a little louder than was necessary. The doctor's eyes remained fixed on his delicate operation.

Gus looked around the office, which seemed almost empty. It contained a wide window overlooking the street, a couple of chairs, the desk, a box on the floor filled with what looked like files, a bucket which acted as a spittoon, and there on a lonely wall, the dubious diplomas. In the corner by the door, a big suitcase stood as if waiting, at a moment's notice, to accompany the good doctor out of town.

The doctor startled him by commanding, "Stand up."

He came around the desk and stood in front of Gus, looking him over. He leaned toward Gus, staring straight into his eyes, until their noses almost touched. The doctor's eyes were like goggles, and his breath was like a swamp. Gus shivered and felt a sneeze approaching. The doctor, anticipating this, rocked back a bit on his heels, still examining Gus' bloodshot eyes.

Gus started to explain about his symptoms and his career, but the doctor cut him short with a curt, "Keep quiet. I'm concentrating."

He put his ear to Gus's chest and listened closely.

"Umm," he murmured. He thumped it with his first two fingers.

"Uh huh," he grunted.

As he walked around Gus, he began muttering to himself. He thumped Gus' back. Gus hoped he knew what he was doing.

"Uh oh," the doctor mumbled.

"Ah ha," he pronounced.

He finished his circling and tapped Gus twice just above the eyes. Gus blinked rapidly. The doctor shook his head.

By this time, Gus was wishing he had gone to see Madame Wanda, the fortune teller, rather than this doctor whose methods seemed just as unfathomable. The doctor resumed his seat behind the desk and stared thoughtfully at Gus, all the while mumbling incoherently to himself. Then, with surprising grace, he spun on his chair to face the window. Gus slowly lowered himself to his own chair.

The doctor continued to mumble. It was as if he were consulting with unseen colleagues. His voice rose and fell. It seemed to put forth one opinion and then, in a different tone, another. It presented, it corrected, it weighed. It balanced, it questioned, it reflected. Gus was so amazed that he almost stopped sneezing.

After several interminable minutes of this dialog, the doctor slammed his palm down on the windowsill. The sudden noise of it made Gus jump and sent him into another attack. Doctor Pedersen turned slowly in his chair to face Gus and began to speak. His tone was grave and had a measured assurance to it, which allowed no room for doubt.

He said, "Son, this is serious and there is no easy way to say it. Based on long experience and my thorough examination, it is obvious to me that you have Terminus Strawfeverus Maximum."

Gus held his breath and blinked his tearing eyes, uncomprehendingly.

The doctor continued, "In other words — Terminal Hay Fever." He looked seriously at Gus.

"Terminal," he repeated, as if this was necessary.

"If you stay here in Minnesota, you will continue to sneeze your brains out, until you reach what will be, I assure you, a very bitter end. I give you about five months."

Gus began to sniffle uncontrollably.

"Your only hope and my recommendation to you is to leave town immediately and go West where the air is different. There is a possibility that you will dry up out there. That these evil vapors will depart. That you might be able to lead a normal life."

He paused to let this sink in.

"It's certain that, by staying here, your days are numbered and your singing career is finished. Go West, young man. It's your only chance. That will be twenty dollars."

Gus fumbled for the money and walked numbly toward the door. Terminus Strawfeverus Maximum!?

Gus turned to the doctor and made a gesture of appeal for some other verdict.

From his seat behind the desk, Doctor Pedersen shook his head solemnly. He lifted his arm and waved his index finger from side to side.

He repeated, "Go West, young man, go West. It's your only chance."

— From *Gus Goes West*

Some blurbs for my books:

Now, I see how to do it. — James Thurber

This guy cracks me up. — Humpty Dumpty

He's got a beard, like me. — Ernest Hemingway

What's a metaphor, anyway? — Herman Melville

So helpful, it's scary. — Edgar Allan Poe

I wish they'd translate this. — Pablo Neruda

What the hell, try it. — Raymond Chandler

Get a pencil, some paper, and a bottle. — F. Scott Fitzgerald

Pretty dramatic, sometimes far-fetched, but quite entertaining.
— Charles Dickens

I read this before I left home. — Thomas Wolfe

The Wonderful World News

Newsletters

Many Wives, Many Masters.

Were you really a king in one of your past lives? I mean, of course, you were. You also had one existence where you got to steer the course of what we now know as, the Ottoman Empire. And then, there was that incarnation, when Cleopatra was begging you to stay the night and yet, you had to break her heart. You bad boy. There was never a time when you were a dog or, even worse, a snail, with a manic condition. No servant appearances or bored farmers. No insect interval, but you may not remember those because of the short life spans.

It's amazing. This stuff happened to everyone. Not one of us is exempt, whether we accept it or not. Some remember, some don't. That's what they say. There is an entire literature and industry devoted to this kind of psychic exploration. Guys will take your there. Induce memories. Regress you by hypnosis. Or just look at you and start revealing your past.

I have dreams, but that's about as psychic as I get. I want all that other stuff to happen - to see the future, be abducted by aliens, and commune with spirits, but it has never happened. I believe it, but I have never had any real experience. Sure, I've hallucinated, but that's different. I want some evidence. Dreaming you are escaping Nazis or Iraqis is not the same thing. There's so much of that on TV and that's just the same as dreaming you're driving a new car.

But every now and then there's something. Something that happens. Someone you meet. And it's not just Deja-vu, which has some perfectly rational explanation that I am not familiar with. You look at them and they're looking at you and you both feel something. I know, you think I'm talking about love or romance or something like that. Well, I'm not. Though she is a woman, she is at least 30 years older than I am and the mother of a friend. Not that I am defensive, but I am not that kind of guy.

This really happened to me and though I'm not sure I can say that this person and I were related in some way in another life, I do know that we both recognized each other. We had a bond. We had an immediate connection and communication with each other. We were soul buddies. The kind of thing it usually takes years to establish.

Stuff like this doesn't just happen. By accident or for the heck of it. You can tell when you are experiencing the miraculous. There is a faint stirring of strings off to the left and goose bumps form on your forearms. Lights flicker and the furnace rumbles.

One time, I met a guy in a bar. I was working, tending bar. We started talking and, though he was drunk (it was his birthday), this was another one of those special times. We were on a similar wavelength. We recognized each other. He was quoting Whitman and telling me about his job as a 'nocturnal boring animal,' setting dynamite charges in tunnels, up in the mountains. He said I should quit my job and go with him to learn how to fish, with sticks or something, from the Indians in Oregon.

Responsible employee that I am/was, I just couldn't do that, but I did toss my apron and vest in the corner and help him celebrate. Was this another visit from a previous existence or merely drinking? I think the former.

I do not like the fact that these encounters are so hard to pin down. So impossible to explain. That there's never time to get down with the other person and try to figure out where you know each other from or what was happening. It's not that they think you're crazy. They don't. They get it. But then it's last call or you're leaving town or they are whisked off by someone, to talk about something completely boring. It's upsetting.

We're talking about something ineffable, ephemeral, almost like a dream, except something that really happens. It's a profound encounter. I miss these guys even if they're from another century. There are plenty of wonderful people in this lifetime, but I hate to lose touch with the people I love.

I am always looking people in the eye, searching for that familiar spirit. That connection, that certainty that ours is a meeting that, in this life, at least, we should celebrate, even if we can't prove it.

You don't run into these guys every day. I think we are so often alone in this world, or, even if we aren't, it's always great to see someone from the old hometown.

Get on the Good Foot!

I am, among other things, a trained and certified Life Coach. It was a lot of work and considerable expense. But I could have avoided all that, because, for years, though I didn't know it, I had been studying at the feet of the master. The ultimate coaching machine. The hardest working man in interpersonal relations. The Godfather of Soul and Personal Transformation — Mister James Brown.

Though, sadly, he is gone, he left behind records of his sessions. In these, his worldly experience, his perceptive and wise, not to mention funky, understanding of human relations is there for all time to help us negotiate the rapids of relationships and the intricacies of individual human development.

Many of his teachings have entered the mainstream and taken their righteous place in the collective unconscious. *Get Up Offa That Thing, Dance and You'll Feel Better.* Now, that is an essential exhortation and understanding from which everyone can benefit.

The legacy he left us is virtually inexhaustible. And it will always be relevant and immediate. For example, put on *I Got the Feeling* and turn up the volume. It is not just an intellectual lesson; it is a somatic one. Just try sitting still clutching the beliefs and self-concepts that no longer match the person you are today. Say the words, I Feel Good. Affirmation is not just some woo woo idea; it's a cathartic explosion. A reprogramming of your internal computer. Embrace the concept. Hold to that vision of what is and what can be.

Mr. James Brown did not find all this in a book. He found it on the road. In small towns and smoky dives and incorporated the lessons learned there until eventually he could consult with auditoriums and arenas full of people who had sought out and intuitively designed a working relationship with this sage from Augusta, GA.

Throughout his career, James Brown championed and challenged the souls of people who were discouraged, confused, who suffered from low self-esteem, and who were at a point in their lives where they were ready for change. James Brown supplied the words that echoed their deepest feelings. His own journey was one of constant questioning and a determination to move forward.

He shared his own struggle in such great songs as: *I'll Go Crazy. Think. Get It Together.* and *Talking Loud and Saying Nothing.* His moments of desperation come through in: *Please, Please, Please. Bewildered. I Can't Stand Myself. I've Got Ants In My Pants.*

As he began to find his way, he shared his inner dialogue of affirmation and encouragement: *Pump Up the Volume. Don't Be a DropOut. You've Got to Change Your Mind.* and *Get Up, Get into It, Get Involved.* He celebrated personal triumph and expressed real joy, when he sang: *You've Got The Power. Papa's Got A Brand New Bag. It's a Brand New Day, So Let A Man Come In And Do The Popcorn. Say It Loud, I'm*_____ (you fill in the blank) *and I'm Proud.*

There's no denying the influence of James Brown. He, in his way, coached a nation at a critical point in its struggle for equality for all its citizens. He provided the keys for self-development. He challenged us to get up offa our things and get it together. As a coach, he provided inspiration and an energy that may never be equaled. Personally, I am indebted to him for his wise counsel and encouragement at important moments of my life and am forever grateful for his example and his determination to never give up or settle for anything less than the best.

Thank you, Mr. Dynamite!

As he said, so often, Get on Up and Get on The Good Foot!

Polka — Curse or Cure-all?

It's a simple matter of heaving your weight to one side, in three short steps. 1 - 2 - 3. Then, to the other side. 1 - 2 - 3. Turn slowly through the six total steps. Repeat endlessly.

Those are the details. The important things about it are girls, music, and beer. The order of these will vary with the circumstances, but isn't it wonderful to be able to combine the three most important things in life into one brief dance?

Let's examine in, cursory, if not excessive, detail these three fundamentals of the good life. Girls — They hold a fascination for a guy like me, not only for the obvious reasons, which I won't go into, aside from noting that they (girls) are warm, soft, and much more discriminating than I am. Yes, this could also be said of kittens, dogs, and all sorts of animals, but have you ever seen any of those doing the Polka?

What really fascinates me about girls is their minds. I swear I am not lying. Their view of the world, their sensitivity, and their imaginations. It's a puzzlement and a wonderment. Plus, many of them can keep time and carry a tune. In Polka, as in Square Dancing, one (me, I) is put in direct contact with this magic. Excitement is inevitable!

The instrumentation of accompaniment can range from full orchestra to quartets, from tubas to saxophones, from guitars to the almost indispensable accordion. The accordion is a versatile and portable instrument that has the added bonus of being able to supply the bass, the beat, and the melody.

Most scoff at the accordion, but throughout the history of the instrument (and it is a long and distinguished, not to mention, romantic one) there have arisen great artists, such as, Frankie Yankovic, Fat Louie Szykowski, and Babe Wagner — all household names. All it takes is a few notes and you know you're in for something special.

Beer, besides being one of the basic food groups, (as necessary to life, some argue, as water) is the lubricant, nay, the WD-40, of Polka. It frees the participants of shyness. It facilitates movement. And it can round off the rough edges of one's inexperience, one's lack of coordination, and make each partner essential to the dream. I won't go so far as to say it is the blood of romance. That's gross and inaccurate, but it helps with dry lips.

These three elements combined, have been known to provide comfort, enable excess, and promote needed exercise. Romance aside, Polka is a workout. But it is one where everyone is smiling and ready for more.

In addition, it can be a poetic expression for sensitive souls. Just take a peek at these Polka titles:

The Fireside Polka   Jolly Wife of Mine Polka
Twenty Flowers Polka   The Ponytail Polka
Hoosier Susie Polka   Mother-in-law Polka
Strip Polka   The Okey Dokey Polka

And who can forget such favorites as:

My Baby's Got A Nice Dupa
The Night Lil' Wally Came to Town
Waukesha, All Praise To Thee!

I have many Polka memories and not just because I'm from Minnesota, a state known for its cultural, intellectual, and musical luminaries. Early morning AM radio, while driving through endless fields of corn, in sunshine or in blizzard. That wedding reception where my girlfriend and I fell into the closet, while trying to retrieve our coats. That old white, clapboard community center, alone, in a forest clearing, up North, and a party just for the hell of it, on a Sunday afternoon.

Some say there is no beer in heaven. Does that mean, by extension, that there is no Polka, either? No one's God could be that cold. But, just in case, I'm getting mine in now.

Rocket Number Nine, take off for the planet... Venus!

I am under attack by an alien being! Everything in the kitchen is turning green. I'm getting desperate. There's no beer, no milk, no chips. The blender screams through the night. The oven is producing things at a frightening rate and I don't understand any of them. You've heard of things growing in the refrigerator. Well, it's worse than that.

My wife wasn't always an alien, and I have the pictures to prove it. But she has recently revealed herself to me as a Vegan. She tells me this will be a good thing for both of us, but that usually means that I'm going to suffer.

My wife loves food and I love her, but my eating habits developed in Minnesota, where, in my formative years, we considered ketchup too spicy and the most ethnic food available was spaghetti, out of a can. My staples were meatloaf, potato chips, and Velveeta. Canned hash, fish sticks, and, if we were really good, some pudding or Jello. Meals, at our house, didn't involve too much thought. In fact, we spent most of them in front of the television.

We were a family who appreciated the basics. I even prepared some of the meals, though I can't say that I learned to cook much. My mother could only make orange juice and angel food cake. I loved those cakes. If we were bad, she'd threaten us with devil's food.

My wife, Mary Liz, as I call her, is a great cook. A master in the kitchen. An adventuress of unquestioned taste. A gourmet and gourmand of the highest order. Give that girl a couple of tomatoes and some leftovers and be prepared to call it divine intervention. Your taste buds will shoot straight to Heaven. People come over to our house and wash dishes, just to be in the same kitchen with her. We have to throw our friends out.

But, here, I must confess something. I have been a trial to her. A burden of under-appreciation. A philistine set beside such sophistication should be criminal. Her finest creations pass by unnoticed. Desserts that have made other men cry, merely fill me up. I can hear her working in the kitchen at this very moment. Preparing an evening feast that I know I can't do justice to.

Why she stays with me is a mystery. Sure, I feel guilty. You would too, if your palate were as limited as mine. I've tried. God knows I've tried to expand my idea of what constitutes a good meal, but now this. This Veganism. This organically correct, this life-affirming, this good for your body and soul way of eating somehow sits there on the plate in opposition to everything that has sustained me thus far. No fats. No dairy. No alcohol.

She loves me and is trying to save me from my history and that is something that pierces my heart. I gaze at her gratefully, with a tear in my eye. But that tear, though a sign of the infinite love I have for her, is also a tear for the end of my youth. A tear for the elements that have made up my foundation and have created the cute roll of fat that hangs over the sides of that foundation. A tear that is a sign that, as a great British philosopher once said, all things must pass. All things must pass away.

But, because of my love and my confidence in her ability to transform even the meanest crumbs, well, not crumbs, unfortunately there is no bread involved in this, but, as I was saying, my love and faith in her ability to transform the greenest, the meanest, the most unlikely organic matter into something fit for a king, because of this I follow in the wake of her wisdom. I take the path that she has embraced and I know, with a certainty not unlike the guarantee that comes with a Honda, that all will be well. Me belly full. She satisfy my soul.

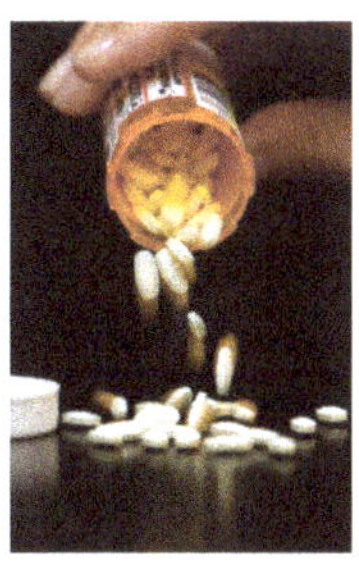

The Attack of the Pharmaceuticals

On those nights when I can muster the courage to watch the news, my expectations are always exceeded. Or is it that my fears are always confirmed? Whatever they are, they consist of a frightened understanding that things might be even worse than the night before. Also present is an unspecified dread that the events they are reporting may have some kind of direct impact on me. Every now and then might be bearable, but night after night?

As disturbing as these reports from around the world are, the commercials shown between the news segments are as, no, are even more disturbing. They not only seem to take up more minutes than the actual news, but they directly relate to my mortality and the general breakdown that my body, like all others, must undergo over time. Personally, that breakdown seems to be gathering momentum. Aches, pains, and problems make themselves known on an ever more frequent basis and they seem to stick around longer.

I've been reading about the Mind-Body Connection and, each night, I see that these drug companies have no interest in helping me. They would rather plant the seed that Arthritis or PAD (whatever that is) is taking root, at this very moment, in my quite vulnerable and susceptible body. Statistics have proven this and you know you can't escape that kind of truth. No matter how special you might think you are today, tomorrow you will be just one more number in a long and indifferent report.

You and your friends will never again be able to be more than thirty yards away from a bathroom. You will have all kinds of trouble going, stopping, getting up in the night, and a lot of other things I don't want to think about. You could be out biking with other gray-haired guys, who never even think about going. Or you could be kayaking miles away from the nearest bathroom. All you have to do is ask your doctor about it. You're there all the time, anyway. Just ask him.

Sure, there are some side effects, but they're not major, only dry mouth, excessive perspiration, sudden seizures, vomiting, runny nose, debilitating muscle spasms, difficulty breathing, dementia, and the ever-present threat of sudden heart attacks, leading to death. Okay! I'm asking!

It used to be that I only needed to be aware of the heartbreak of Psoriasis or an occasional blinding headache, but just as things are deteriorating in the Middle East, so are they deteriorating right here at home. At my house. In my bed. Inside me!

I never used to have any of these problems. I could go for walks without suffering blocked arteries. My allergies never bothered me. Heck, I didn't even have any. And, though not a Casanova, I have always thought of myself as a local Don Juan. But now, I know that I am part of the growing (if I may use that word) E.D. population. I find myself envious of guys I would have laughed at before. I see that they have fulfilling relationships with people they are actually married to, and many of them have matching bathtubs! By the ocean!

Each day, my list of problems grows. I can't keep up with all of them. I think it's safe to say that there is no part of me that isn't diseased. My eyes are dry, my joints ache. I might have Athlete's Foot. Sometimes my stomach is upset and full of gas, my blood can't circulate properly, my levels are low, my blood pressure is high, I'm often disoriented, and I could have a heart attack, at any moment.

I can't think about the News. I've got a lot more problems than that. No wonder I'm depressed. Maybe there's something I can take for that.

Earth Day!

It's a quantum thing. That's what we say around our house. As far as I can tell, it means that the observation of an object affects its condition. This act of observation affects or changes its reality. That means that as a result of what your beliefs are, in combination with your intention and the intensity of both, you can affect the reality of an object or a person or a situation. This is in addition to whatever actions you are taking.

Through rigorous experimentation, this quantum kind of activity has been proven true. This revolutionizes our scientific understanding of reality. Scientists know this stuff, and have for a while, but it is now reaching a wider public. Guys, like myself, whose understanding of physics is based on shooting pool or trying to fix things around the house, are finally becoming acquainted with these ideas. And, about time, my wife says.

It's wonderful. Just when things were beginning to seem incredibly bleak, dark, and despairing, we find out that each one of us has the power to affect whatever we turn our thoughts to. Saints and sages have told us this from the start, but I always thought it was wishful thinking, a matter of faith, and more than a little beyond my reach. Now, with this scientific corroboration, a wider, more brilliantly lit set of possibilities is revealed.

I'm not going to use this knowledge for trivial things, like toasting bagels or making my television larger. I'm not even going to use it for personal gain. No, I want to use it for the big stuff: the things that affect all of us. The things I have, up to this time, felt were out of my hands —

war and peace, disease and poverty, ignorance and disastrous climate change. It has now been proven, by hard-working people in white coats, toiling in cramped office space at our great universities and in garages everywhere, that optimism and directed intense visualization of a desired outcome can actually make things change.

We, each of us, have a part to play in this life, a part that has meaning and actual effects. That is an amazing thing and, understanding it, creates an opportunity and responsibility we never knew we had.

There are many areas and issues that are in need of our attention. The most timely and most crucial, to me, seems to be the state of the Environment, the health of our planet, this wonderful world we all inhabit. It is now generally recognized that we are in a dire situation. To mention just a few areas of concern, we have melting ice caps, air pollution, radical changes in weather patterns, a declining supply of fresh water, and the disappearance of bees. I don't want to look up at the sky and feel afraid. I want us to have the peace of mind to think about other things like how beautiful the flowers are or how we might help someone not as lucky as we are or how we can assist our kids' imagination, compassion, and forward momentum.

We can use this quantum stuff as one way to affect the world with our hearts and minds, applying our intention and energy and emotion to make things better for all of us. This Earth, this big old ball of blue, this beautiful whirling dervish that we live on, needs our help. We're smarter now. We understand the situation. And we're not powerless. That's the lesson of Earth Day. We can realize a consciousness we didn't know we had before and end the shortsightedness that has been causing us so much pain.

I'm going to try it out. And keep trying until I get it right. Happy Earth Day! Go outside. Take a deep breath. Celebrate. It's difficult to deny reality, but we *can* change it.

Are You Okay?

Are you feeling faint? Are you experiencing a slight gnawing in your stomach? Is everything becoming dim?

Ask yourself, 'Just how long has it been since I sent a check to my friend, Ringer?' If you find that it has been longer than twelve months or even if it's only been two weeks, why not send ten dollars to ensure the health and continuation of your subscription to the Wonderful World News?

This muttering of scratches, on soon to be recycled paper, needs your support and seldom solicits it actively. But it is at this very moment.

If you desire to be completely free forever of the symptoms mentioned above, why not get a lifetime subscription for $100? It can be passed on to your heirs in the event of your transformation.

Send all your checks to:

Ringer
733 Sunset Street
Longmont, CO 80501

Thanks.

Back at the Glamorama

I used to have a TV. When I had it, I only watched nature shows on PBS or Sixty Minutes. I was a responsible viewer. Sure, on rare occasions, I'd get up on Saturday mornings and watch Pee Wee's Playhouse and, later, I'd tune in a game. During the week you might find me early mornings, stretching in the company of several very fit women. Later, the Today Show and some guy with a mustache would bring me reports from the social battleground. At night I watched serious, dramatic programs. And, of course, the weather. When I had a free moment and wanted to relax, I watched old cartoons and now and then caught a glimpse of Sponge Bob. But not often. I was a responsible viewer.

My Early Training

I was brought up on TV. Andy and Aunt Bea took care of me. I spent my vacations with Tarzan and Jane. Beaver was my little brother. Not really. But it seemed that way. I watched Romper Room, Howdy Doody, The Mickey Mouse Club and, later, the Galloping Gourmet. These shows helped shape my view of the world.

College introduced me to more fulfilling pastimes like Frisbee, beer, and sleeping. As a result, I cut my TV watching to a minimum. Just what was needed to be an informed citizen — knowledgeable about current events, stock market analysis, and the latest fashion trends.

A Serious Viewer

Yes. I was a serious viewer with one exception — the soap operas. This was the place where real life and complete fantasy intersected. The characters seemed just like me and my neighbors. Continuous intrigue, infidelity, and vanity. But on TV, it was more exciting, and you were able to find out about everyone's adventures. And it was always their problem.

It was fertile ground for the student of human relations and, as one, I found myself, sandwich in hand, in front of the set. I was on the edge of my couch, each day, as the soaps spun their webs. They drove me wild. Over time, they began to interfere with my modest ambitions, my meals, my life.

In desperation, I began to keep the set in the closet. I promised that I would only bring it out for earthshaking events. Soon however, it was back in its old place in front of the couch. In the end, I knew I had to free myself. I passed my set on to others who could still watch responsibly.

No More TV

I'm glad I don't have a TV anymore. Its absence allows me the time and energy for other (more important?) activities such as mowing the lawn, doing the dishes, and writing these newsletters.

But every now and then, usually as I'm trying to fall asleep, I wonder whatever happened to Adam and to what new depths Tad has sunk. Last night, I experienced a moment of weakness. Sleep was impossible. I went to the supermarket and bought a copy of Soap Opera Weekly. Immediately, I was brought up to date on the latest developments. Here is a look at some of my favorite soaps and what transpired this past week.

The Merest Thread

We threw ourselves over the precipice of love and now our lives hang by... The Merest Thread.

Carlos discovers Anita in the garage polishing the car. John reveals to Eve his sex change operation of six years ago, while in the Navy.

Laurie breaks off her engagement with Louis when she learns of his 'Night School' activities. Michelle is arrested for Murder One and is smitten by Officer Edwards. A. J. spends his entire life savings on lottery tickets to pay for Annie's surgery. Brooks realizes that he is over his head when he comes upon Holly and Heather in the garden.

Another World

They loved like us (well, maybe a little better), but they came from... Another World.

Jodie confides in Roberta that she still loves David, despite his obsession with Helen's handbag. Roberta tells Jodie it's not Helen anymore, it's Carolyn. Brad and Tina make love at the laundromat. Simon can't believe it when he learns of Trudi's origins, especially when she tells him that it is his fault. Gavin contacts the home planet and complains about his assignment.

Des Moines

There's no place like home and our home is... Des Moines.

Bob and Ellen drop by his parent's house for dinner. Barbara, Bob's mom, reveals her secret recipe for meatloaf to Ellen who is shocked to realize that it is identical to her own mother's recipe. Billy arrives home, late from school, smelling like perfume. Ellen decides to call her mother. June and Tom go out to the farm for a weekend alone. Donna borrows the car and tells her mom that she is meeting Kim at the mall. She goes straight to Jim's clubhouse.

Fit To Love

Those who shape themselves through effort and purpose are better people for they are... Fit To Love.

Simon spies Terri in the weight room and asks if she wants to join him in the sauna. Her earbuds prevent her from hearing him and she mistakenly assumes he knows about her and Tony. She confesses everything. Flushed from her workout, Karen meets mysterious Mr.

Frederick, the new member. When Mark finds his love for Amy unrequited and his pulse racing, he does three classes in a row and is taken to the hospital. Steve learns of Jock's indiscretion in the locker room. Lauren and Paul meet each morning in stretching class but are both too shy to reveal their bodybuilding passion.

These Idle Moments

We live for tomorrow, but first... These Idle Moments.

While in line at the Post Office, Suzanne tells Carol that Mario has been making love to her daughter during his lunch hour. Kevin's fantasies are revived while waiting for the stoplight on Pine Street. Tiffany and Brent are shocked to find that there is a forty-five minute wait at Juanita's. At the dentist's office, Elliott pretends to be reading the magazines, but is actually undressing the receptionist in his mind. Tracy goes over her list, once more, while on hold for Arthur.

All This and More

We have more than we need but there's still some left. We can have... All This and More.

During dinner at the Farrington mansion, Vanessa drops Alex the bomb that she is expecting his baby in three weeks. Vanessa cries when Alex admits he doesn't remember her and then leaves. Robin wonders if she and Andrew should get another credit card. Cynthia hijacks the plane on her way home from Barbados and demands that they fly her to Jamaica. George, devastated by Nancy's revelation that she loves the postman, tries to kill himself by eating six rolls of stamps. Trevor's wallet has partially paralyzed him causing Connie, who was upset already, to seek out the doctor. Susan receives a letter from Ted that explains everything.

Into the Future

Meet George Jetson. Jane, his wife. Everyone is smiling. We're levitating. Or our food is. Robots are everywhere and they're smiling. I can't wait to get there.

Back in the Twentieth Century, we adolescent boomers had not only the world before us, but the future, too. There were no limits to what would be accomplished and everyday would be better than the one before.

The future would hold no end of surprises and improvements. That future would open out limitlessly and, at the end of it, somewhere, was a rainbow or the largest ice cream cone in the universe or something way beyond what we could even begin to imagine. No matter what, it was going to be good. It was exciting.

I'm not so sure, anymore. Have I just gotten older or did something else happen that changed that view?

At my core, I still feel that way - there are no limits to what can be accomplished and there are people, just like me, who are discovering, developing, and creating a future that is exciting and good for everyone.

But something feels different. I used the phrase — *in the future* — in a letter yesterday and could feel that change. The words are the same, but my idea of the future has been tempered by gray hair, traffic, and weather.

Time passes and, though relative, it's also, for each of us, finite. As the possibility, the probability, and finally, the inevitability of an end becomes a reality, my idea of the future has undergone a radical change.

But there's more to it than just my mortality. The population has increased and all those initial realizations and forecasts that had recently begun to surface, when I was young, have become fact. Statistics, though open to interpretation, signal overload. Resources, employment, and psychological stability are under tremendous pressure.

Systems of all sorts and the biggest one of them all — the ecological system — are failing and not moving toward that brighter future. War, political conflict, the decline of natural resources, an outdated educational process, and attacks on reason cast a pall over many things.

This is not the exciting future I was expecting. Where are all the smiling robots? I can see now that the older model of the future I had was a passive one. Inaccurate. Unrealistic. I thought the future would stop at the corner and pick me up as it went by. It may be the passing of time or because of all the information that's available, but I know now that things don't work that way.

The future is, and always has been, a function of choice. A function of our individual efforts and imagination. We actually get to choose what that future will be. What each of us does with our time here matters. Our actions determine that future. We can learn from the past and imagine what we want to happen next. We can put our energy behind that. We can see it in whatever way we want.

We can feel what makes us uncomfortable and what makes us hopeful. That's a choice that shouldn't be that complicated. Stop or go? Give up or try? Despair or hope? What feels good or what feels bad? Forget about what is possible or not. We won't know until we try.

The future I want to participate in, exist in, walk into, move into, claim as my own, is one that sparkles. The one that starts again each day. The one I/we get to make. Not the one I'm afraid is going to happen, but the one I want to happen.

In the future, everything will still be a surprise and beyond my imagination, but it will be one that I have a hand in creating. That's my choice. How this future comes together will always be a mystery, a conundrum, a paradox. It's the micro and the macro. Individual and inclusive. Here today and here tomorrow. I can't worry about that.

I'm letting go of that old future. I've got a choice and I'm making it. I'm making the future right now. Come on over and we can create it together.

Every two weeks I go to the cancer place. Up two flights to the infusion center. As far as I know, it's like that flavored vodka or tea, except that they infuse me with something that comes out of a needle.

I've been doing this for years. There are others there who also just walk in, but then they have to stay there, connected to tubes infusing something much more potent than what I'm getting. Their situation is infinitely more serious than mine and, often, they don't have one year, let alone more.

I'm kind of a drive-by in that I sign in, wait a couple of minutes until Anne or Michelle or Don come by and poke me in the arm. Then, I'm free to go. Everyone is as nice as can be and they have even provided snacks for the patients to tide them over and to settle their stomachs.

I'm usually there around lunch and, sometimes, I see the snack cart with its goodies and check out the selection. Most of it is of no interest, but this week I saw the shiny blue wrapper of a pack of Oreos. I looked around and slipped one of the packages into my pocket, unseen. I'm both six and about sixty when I do this.

Out in the car, once I've left the parking lot, I read on the blue wrapper that this is America's Favorite Cookie. That's certainly true in this moment.

I separate the halves to better enjoy the filling, as I wonder what else I can learn to love like Oreos.

Grow Old with Me

Death. We can only really think of it as a slow progression to a foggy, if not unconscious, end. An end we can't really believe, because end has always meant the end of one thing and the start of another.

But sometimes this end is unexpected. Sudden. Shocking. Violent. Many years ago, John Lennon was shot and killed. A young guy, a fan, walked up to him at the front door of his apartment building and shot him. Twice. A suddenly violent end for someone who had always sung about love. Or peace. Or imagination. John, too much a part of us all to call Lennon, was with Yoko. They had been inseparable, except for the lost weekend or whatever they call it, for 12 years. Companions, collaborators, man and wife. An island of two in a sea of hype, flashbulbs, and gossip.

They were walking home, returning from recording what would become the songs, *Just Like Starting Over* and *Grow Old with Me. Our life together is so precious together, We have grown, God bless our love.* These are just some of the lyrics. The meaning, the emotion was not of a moon in June, but an unadorned feeling of joy, gratitude, and love. Not a story, not just lyrics that rhymed, but a personal statement of something between two real people, artists, who having lived it and made it a part of themselves, wanted to share this with the world.

Starting over, they were looking forward. Grow old with me – this was a hope, a realization of the preciousness of life, an acceptance and appreciation of something real and beautiful. But then death interrupted, violently. Senselessly and yet unbelievably real. A split second unalterably changing the course of many things.

And, for us, it had a different meaning. It was a collective experience, though of a similar sadness. It was a reminder of the delicate hold we have on life. Each step on the Earth a fragile gift, a momentary possibility, a starting over, a deep desire to grow old together, hoping the end will arrive in good time, after we realize we have had it all.

Here's My Advice

Ignore your baser instincts. Resist the calls of couch, television, and distraction. Fight for what you recognize as best for you. Don't be tempted by fate (or what passes for it), outdated responses and beliefs, or the siren songs of situation comedy, celebrity lifestyles, and elusive fashion. Avoid the reruns, pay no attention to the men behind the curtain, stop listening to Rod Stewart, the Eagles, and Billy Joel. Shade your eyes against the glare of fear and imagine that heaven is here, in this moment, and that you have a part to play in creating it. Sing the praises of ornithology, a good cheeseburger, and a beer. Celebrate the jokes of your friends, their heartaches, and their hopes for tomorrow. Create a new tune to be carried forth by bees, buddies, and the next email. Declare a holiday. Insist on goodness. Lead a cheer for discovery. Demand honesty. Manifest imagination. Encourage new species. Stimulate excitement. Inspire reality. Rally the downhearted. Awaken longing and expectation. Revive forgotten dreams. Embrace the moment and each other. Empathize with the flowers. Embody what you want to see. Assemble like-minded amateurs. Harness the energy of willingness. Emphasize the melody. Discontinue guilt, shame, and embarrassment. Defy tradition. Unite all hope. Bring about cooperation. Holler at the headlines. Accommodate the paradox. Revise the paradigm. Present the forgotten and disregarded. Soothe the savage feast. Entreat the blank facades. Shake up the sediment. Juxtapose the isolated. Humor the humorless. Open all doors and windows. Call forth all secrets. Clarify the clutter. Respect the elders. Respect experience. Listen for clues. Hand out ideas and inspirations as if they were candy. Guide the innocent. Disarm the grumpy. Take hold of each other. Greet grief with understanding and patience. Generate passion. Benefit the benevolent. Kickstart the kindness. Glean all joy and focus it. Enervate the doodad. Exult the whim-wham. Elevate the knick-knack. Let geegaws flourish.

Questions, Questions, Questions

They're everywhere. When they get together, they multiply. Once put into motion, they take on a life of their own and it appears there is no end in sight. How big can a question get? Is a profound question more demanding than one that is casually dressed? And who is to say which is which? Isn't everything relative, anyway? And won't an excess of questions drive us crazy?

How can we possibly sort them all out? There seems to be no stopping them. Just when you think you've answered plenty for one guy or have finally set them aside for good and gone about your business, here comes another one.

First, from birth, there's — when's lunch? A bit later, it's why am I going to school? Sure, there's learning and everything, but then you wonder about issues of control and conformity, not to mention the rationale for authority. Why can't I say that? Why can't I go outside? And, perhaps more importantly, what's her name?

Dion said it best, Why must I be a teenager in love? It's a bittersweet moment for these teenagers and will lead to other questions that lay the groundwork for a process they call maturation. This maturation has its own set of questions, such as, who am I? Why am/are I/we here? (What!?), and who are you? This is the beginning of a personal philosophy.

This process of maturation and the development of a personal philosophy can take a while. I guess it all depends on when you want to stop or when you've had enough and you just can't take it any longer.

After you've settled the serious question of How am I going to make any money, you tackle ones like, Is marriage possible? Or even desirable? That maturity issue keeps poking its head into things and asks, am I really ready or responsible enough for that kind of thing? And then, what about kids?

A bit later, while looking in the mirror, you turn to your wife and ask, am I getting older? She looks at you, with sympathy. You begin to notice things that bring up questions of their own: What happened? Where are those hairs disappearing to? Do I really look like my dad? And then, the David Byrne question, how did I get here?

My own maturation process tells me that many of these questions I'm talking about are Male-specific. And it's true. I have no idea what questions women are asking themselves. Which brings up another question, why are they so different? Not that I mind. I'm glad they are, but they're a mystery.

Some questions just won't go away, no matter how many times you think you've answered them. Who do I think I am? Or, rather, who am I? What is this world all about? Why are things the way they are? What should I do? What's the best use of my time? Sometimes it's, Are you kidding me? The number and scope of questions is limitless. Which begs the question, why me?

I've found that it's a good plan to pay attention, but to always go with the flow. My favorite question is the one that asks, what exciting thing is going to happen next?

Answers are hard to come by, but there's always another question.

Words. Wurds. Wudz.

I love them. I need them. I revel in them. I juggle them like ripened pears on a day glistening with the sunshine of a thousand years. Wait a minute! I apologize. Carried away, again. The deal is: there are so many of them. They represent opportunity, but also confusion. Some, like Bam, for instance, seem inevitable and obvious, but I can't think of many like that. Most are arbitrary, or, if not, way beyond any logical origin I can figure out.

Take, chair. Does that look like a chair? Sure, but you knew that. You could just as easily have called it table, or fire truck.

One step below usage lies madness. So, for our purposes today, let's dispense with reason. Kind of sounds intriguing. The fact that we're using words to describe all of this is hurting my head. What I really want to do is to point out the sounds of some words that may provoke wonder, bafflement, even experimentation. Or a million other things. You just can't tell with words.

If you were me, you would realize, 1. How hard it is to stop writing not only useful, but unusual words. 2. How thinking like this might drive you crazy. 3. The philosophical, if not practical, dilemma initiated by a question like Why? or how chaos is created by subtracting meaning from a perfectly good system of communication.

Consider the following words as words, as sounds, as objects without definition. It's an example of focusing our attention, like a microscope, on a part of something and not being able to recognize it. Okay, okay. Enough.

Gazebo Bingo Pluto
Jello Honcho Bongo
Bamboo Kazoo Wahoo
Whoop de do

See what I mean? And it's not just the ones that end in O, though that does add a bit of fun. That's simply a function of the suffix, O. None of these words are really related.

How about words like:

Smock Aplomb Pizza
Keel Bunch Urchin
Orbit Swank Rash

As objects, they are interesting. As sounds, they are evocative. Let's mess around.

"Keel your swank orbit, my little pizza. That smock seems wahoo honcho. Could gazebo bingo the bamboo from aplomb?"

This is getting good.

"A rash bongo led the jello to a safe urchin. In Kazoo, we bunch."

And so on.

Words. Wurds. Wudz. They intoxicate. They reduce me to tears. They inspire the ineffable. They illuminate the elusive. They call us to action. They are a smock bunch. They orbit the jello. Who knew the rash gazebo? Remember the whoop de do!

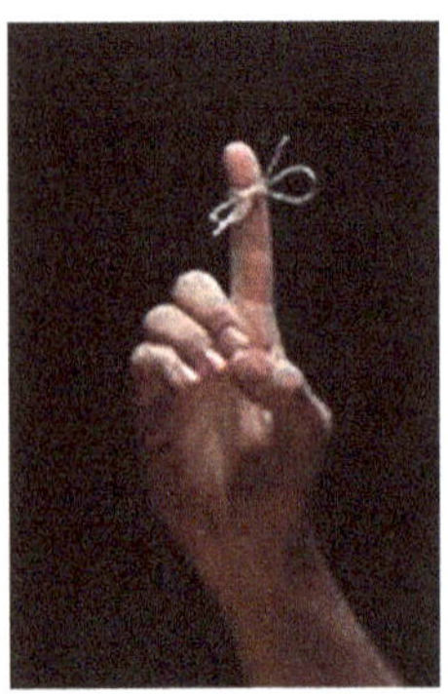

Say What?

There's something important I want to say about memory. Wait a minute... Oh yeah, memory is no joke. Or, joking about its deterioration and loss is not funny and, it may well be that joking might actually pave the way for this downhill slide.

Okay, I'm getting older. I bet you are, too. They say our memories begin to decline around age thirty. They are talking about our ability to remember, not about the quality of those memories. Somehow, everything was fine until recently. Who cared? I never was good with names. Or numbers. It was when I started to react to my image in the mirror, with shock and despair, and began to notice all the old guys around me, that I began to wonder if there had been something I had forgotten.

I've never been particularly organized and misplacing something, like my keys, or having to look for something, like my checkbook, just seemed like a normal thing. And, it still may be, but these occurrences, coupled with what I know about aging and memory, are beginning to make me wonder.

Our world is, without doubt, a busier, more crowded place than ever before. The world population doubles, let's say, every fifty years. How can I possibly remember all those names? The internet has made all information available all the time. This is a wonderful thing in many ways, but how am I supposed to know and remember all of it?

As a young man with a good education, I felt that I knew, or if I applied myself, could learn almost everything important about everything. Now, I see how wrong I was. How naïve. It may have been possible, at one time, maybe, in the 1790s, but no more. That's fine, but I'm getting a complex about it. Perhaps, it's wrong to see it like this, but I feel it's a failing of some sort. It makes me question what I do know. And what is it I do know? I can't remember, but I'm confident that when a situation and context come up and call for this knowledge, I will be able to respond.

I like to think I'm living in the moment. That, with my years of experience, I have acquired wisdom and self-reliance and confidence, but, maybe, it's really an increasing ignorance. A bliss disguised as a moment of enlightenment. An example of a void, instead of restraint.

After all, every one of us gets older. We decline. We enter our dotage. We are not as nimble as we once were. We find ourselves on the outside of the important activities of the world and in a more observational role. We are commenting on things from that mountaintop of our accumulated knowledge, experience, and wisdom. We now focus more on inner, rather than outer events and nuances. Nuances like, where are those keys? And did I leave my checkbook somewhere? Who is that in the mirror? And what was I watching before this commercial?

I like to think that it is all a matter of attention. You remember things that are important to you. You pick and choose where you place that attention, based on your tried and trusted judgment. Many of the things that I was consumed with before, no longer seem important. They no longer merit my interest. Like, love handles or scrutinizing every word that leaves my mouth.

Things that concerned me before, now fall away and I have a more philosophical view of memory. If I can't recall the name of my wife's cousin, it's not a sign of dementia, it's just that I am interested in something else. When I can't remember my wife's name, then I'll get concerned.

After all, I don't want to spend my life worrying about what I do and do not remember. I want to spend it in this moment. With what's her name.

Holidays

Any Excuse to Celebrate.

January 1. Now.

This is it! A New Year! A new day! Just in time for right now.

I love these years. No matter what I do or don't do, whether I'm here or in outer space, on the bus or not, in my right mind or otherwise, driving on the right or left, sinking or swimming, here or there, or everywhere, Time does just what it's supposed to. There's no need to make holidays last all week. No, just for the heck of it, having only weekends during the summer. No switching the months around to see what might happen. Time is something we can count on. It's a linear progression. You can dance to it.

Each new year, each new day, we are given a chance to get it right. To make things work out. To speak our minds and lead with our hearts. To remember what we don't want to forget. To take the next step. To keep moving. To kiss and make up. To keep on the sunny side. To look for the silver lining. To breathe deeply. To smell the roses. To go where no man has gone before. To Do Wah Diddy.

You've got to admit, we are the lucky ducks on this pond. So, no need to hesitate. Simply go ahead on. See what's around the corner.

Grab a partner. Take it from the top. And sing out on the chorus.

Roses Are Red

Oh, Sweetheart, be mine.

It's hard to argue with that. Each February, in the midst of the desolate, the cold, the long wait for spring, I start thinking about Valentine's Day. Or, as it used to be known, St. Valentine's Day.

St. Valentine. What a guy. He was a martyr for love. That's about the limit for a romantic. Valentine's Day is celebrated around the world.

One billion cards are sent each year, with all kinds of messages. Some are eloquent, some plainspoken. Many simply say, "I love you." Or, as we say it in Danish, "Jeg elsker dig?"

I also like the way these guys say it:

Hawaiians - "Aloha wau ia oi"
Italians - "Ti amo."
Portuguese - "Eu amo te." (Pronounced, eiu amu chee.)
Zulus - "Mena tanda wena."

However you say it, the meaning is clear, direct, and simple. As a great philosopher, Wayne Fontana, once told his buddies, The Mindbenders, *It started long ago In the Garden of Eden, When Adam said to Eve, "Baby, you're for me!"*

For the sake of fairness, I will mention that there exists an anti-Valentine movement. Antivalentinism. That's harsh. It's populated by a bunch of curmudgeons who, because of all sorts of misunderstandings, have closed themselves off from love and, in an effort to fend off loneliness (and, perhaps, madness), have banded together and are thoroughly grouchy.

In yesterday's news, I read that the Saudi's Commission for the Promotion of Virtue and the Prevention of Vice (CPVPV) had forbidden the color red throughout the country. Those guys don't get it. A rose in any other color would be as sweet and all they've done is to create a black market for red roses.

It's a measure of our true inclinations that we have a holiday that celebrates love. No matter how many cards there are or how many flowers are sent, it's impossible to commercialize love.

The beloved poet, Willie Bryant, once said,

Love is beautiful
So gorgeous and divine
Feels like a thousand Mickey Mouses
Running up and down your spine

So, Baby, my Sweetie, my Dear, my One and Only Love, let it be me.

The New York Times Best Sellers

February 14, 2026

An authoritatively ranked (you're telling me) list of books sold in the United States. Sorted by whim, with vigor.

1. **Yearn? Sure, I Yearn** 43 WEEKS ON THE LIST
   by Pauline Dobson Lemonais
2. **The History of Infatuation** 9 WEEKS ON THE LIST
   by Dr. Dorothy Francis
3. **Hearts Galore!** NEW THIS WEEK
   by Colleen Loveman
4. **Excessive Zeal** 5 WEEKS ON THE LIST
   by Cindi Morrison
5. **Love In the Mud** 76 WEEKS ON THE LIST
   by Henry Sweetman
6. **Highland Fling** 2 WEEKS ON THE LIST
   by Lucia di Lammermoor
7. **You Might Get Over It** 12 WEEKS ON THE LIST
   by Evelyn Hugo
8. **Global Amorousity** 32 WEEKS ON THE LIST
   by Eunice Fool
9. **Inferno of Fondness** 34 WEEKS ON THE LIST
   by Charmaine de Lamay
10. **Mrs. Barker's Romance of the Kitchen** 63 WEEKS ON THE LIST
    by Betty Barker
11. **Love you, Man.** NEW THIS WEEK
    by Carl Melonhosen
12. **Euphemisms Of Love** 14 WEEKS ON THE LIST
    by Julie Ann Johnson
13. **My Ardent Epiphany** 41 WEEKS ON THE LIST
    by Sylvia Hottentotter
14. **Love Lost and Found** NEW THIS WEEK
    by Teddy Teakettle

Valentine

The last time you laughed
A world more difficult than this
Relaxed its haunted form
And let passion flash full
Drunk with the night and
Made mad with rhythm

Our open hearts filled
With a sweet song
So ripe and warm
So soft and deep
That every wild rose could imagine its soul
Changed from ancient dream to new symbol

4/20

Put that in your pipe
And smoke it

Thanksgiving

I give my thanks to
A gay and innocent spirit
Stopped cold before its time
So far in the past as to be
Indistinguishable from story
Mistaken for Myth
Confused by history and
Grown vague with distance
Yet, in this moment,
Saved from the infinite nothing
By the elemental pull of my heart
And the continued surprise
Of the present

Advent

Like the friendly snowflakes falling,
so softly, so gently,
no two alike,
may this New Year bring
a joy, unique and wonderful,
to your heart.

Christmas

It's snowing. The lights are up. The tree is decorated. Everyone is hurrying to find just the right thing for just the right person. Music plays everywhere.

Bells are ringing, voices join together, and Stratocasters bend Xmas notes, while Bing and Tony and just about anyone who can sing and a lot of others who (like myself) repeatedly attempt it, no matter the results, go forth spreading the spirit in grocery stores, in mega shopping palaces, at the post office, in drugstores, and even outside in the parking lot.

It's easy to let the commercialism of it all make me crazy, but I won't go into that rant at this time. I try to transform the sounds and sights into something greater than chaos and, at the same time, remember what's absolutely basic to this holiday that, each year, seems to spiral out of control.

That's probably it. Every year, it's wild and out of control. I need to learn to throw all the intentions and wishes and presents and traffic and interpretations and aggravations and limitations up in the air, like confetti or snowflakes, and try to dig it all, because no matter what, there's a spirit.

Christmas is a long (and growing longer) season of anticipation and hope that culminates in a comparatively short time around the tree or by the fire or in my chair or wherever I find myself. This is a moment when everything stops, and a huge emotion makes itself known. All this hubbub has prepared me well and I can feel the underlying spirit of Christmas in its pure form and not be overwhelmed. I find that I'm digging it, while it's happening, just as Frank Zappa advised.

Right then, each year, I make a resolution to bring a little of it with me into the New Year and add it to all the bits I've received from the wonderful Christmases that have come before.

Happy Holidays!!!

Naughty
and nice!
www.bumpersticker.guru

Poems to Soothe the Savages

A Gesture to Exercise

My gesture to exercise
I call it.
This ride I take
each evening, lately.
The dust rises behind me,
I imagine,
as I pedal by.
The hills stretch south
in a long line,
softened by the changing light
and comforted by the
blue of the fading day.

God knows I need the exercise,
but it is the quiet view,
so vast and so still,
horizon to horizon,
that really brings me here.
Clouds hang weightless
above the green and gold
of the prairie
and, if I'm lucky,
I'll see a hawk
on his way home,
like I am,
with the space and time
to feel how lucky he is.

First, we take a little step
And then we take another
We started somewhere way back there
And now we're here, oh brother!

Two Thousand Nine, April fifth
It sounds like science fiction
We're walking on this road of life
Let's do it with conviction

Those little steps accumulate
And take us quite a distance
Along the way, we sometimes fight
But we bow to Time's insistence

There is no other way we find
And no other way is better
We stick our toe into the lake
And each day just get wetter

Finally, we're in the swim
Contentedly, we're floating
Each drop contains a universe
Each drop deserves our noting

Fatman's Prayer

Thank God for clothes.

End of Summer

It's raining cats and dogs,
somewhere.
Here, it only sounds like rain,
someone's sprinkler teasing
the parched blades of grass,
while a hot wind stirs the leaves,
crisp in their desperation.

Dust rises at the passing of a car
choking the slower ones
and a whiff of smoke
predicts trouble to come,
not the tasty snack
near each one's heart.

Heat is not an emotion,
but anger is and
the dream of flowers
has gone up in flames.

Keeping Them Crossed

I cross my fingers
Hope for the best
Indulge in expectation, again
Thinking that knocking on wood
Will protect us all
Or that the proper placement of objects
Will bring about what I am
Always working toward

I send wishes to the stars
And trust that the
Cosmic arrangement of things
Out in cold, dark, and
Unconscious space
Will guide my small dreams
Into orbit around a glowing globe
Somewhere

My intentions are directed
Towards a future I'm hoping
Is beyond the reach of this past
Filled, as it is, with
Cracks beneath my slow-witted feet
Mirrors broken by accident
Hats thrown casually on beds
And a lot of ladders

Idyll

I walk from the house
Up the steep hill and into the woods
Never having been here before

I see the sunlight sift down past
The white birches
Making the tall grass come alive
As I wade through it
Toward a new world

In the light and the breeze
And the greenness of everything
It seems as if time has stood still
And is content to stay that way

An Aesop Fable

There once was a kid named rover
Who wanted to roll in the clover
He thought if he waited
And just contemplated
He'd be in it before it was over

This Rover was unrealistic
And couldn't help going ballistic
When he found it was true
That to get one must do
Then he sighed, he was quite fatalistic

His end was no good, people said
With no will but to lie on his bed
And although it was strange
He kept expecting a change
And he got it, for then he was dead

The Always

I will always want the always
The sense that here is now and for forever
That souls do not depart
That hope can be renewed
That answers can be found
That love is never lost
That doubt is left behind us
And the new is yet to be

An easy code this, to hack or crash or
Light up the screen
With smart memes and cloud phasers
Interface with the almost alien geek wars
Create some online bot upgrade that will stun

Your world is my password
Not for galactic evil
But there in the name of digital
Love, speed, and intelligent
Filing of the system network tech
We need to scream joy and utility

Download never   Upload always

From *Magnetic Poetry*

Checking It Twice

Make a list of the
powerful words
the evocative ones
the ones that will
bring forth love
from the cruelest heart
and replace the weeds
with flowers
that will turn the moon full
that will cast long shadows
that will inspire birdsong
that will ignite the flames
that will melt the ice
set the table
keep the pages turning

that will breathe honey
that will create a breeze
that will still chaos
that will cross bridges at twilight
improve tans
straighten desks
and build strong bodies twelve ways

Words that will saw a woman in half
pull a rabbit out of the hat
push worry to one side
unseal fate
instill confidence
and bind together all wounds

Words that coast downhill and
incite perpetual motion
that carry the tune
take the weight off
induce laughter

Words that bring about reconciliation
accomplish big deeds
that fire the imagination
that initiate long years of prosperity
and cause dreams to arise
like fish to the surface

Words that compel the impossible
install, nearby, the unreachable
and allow the inevitable

Words that
share the wealth
save the whales
and give peace a chance

Words
more powerful than despair
words that evoke the once hoped for
and now forgotten

These words are a way to
define a wish
to tell the future
to make hope real

They're a way to imagine
a place to begin

Counting

Death has its own arithmetic
and the answer is always the same.
And yet, how hard we struggle
To prove it untrue.
In this moment, I prefer ignorance
An optimism that, I think,
Denies reality, but which, in fact,
If I would only acknowledge it,
Embraces the moment, in celebration,
And leaves the inevitable
To its own calculations.

In Awah Dah

Neek woo ze naybah. Moko no feenah zu.
In Hala Eeva, zu wah so fine. We nui
Za badah. E go like dis:

On a day so near le fah
A goo du ga me see so lah
A goo no me ah oh so sweet
De fu she no da nui neet
Dos lips sa wah nee fata yah
She so be sah in awah dah

Tu eetah oos a wah no fah
Me cuus she sah so nee no wah
See scoooo in Hu no fah dee bah
Ah gi woo she ah gi no bah

In The Night

In the time before the light
In the dark, the dark of night
Resting there between the sheets
We try so hard to get our sleep

But the bed is stiff, it's like cement
We twist, we turn, and we lament
We can't slow our thoughts, they're in a torrent
Our future's dim, our life abhorrent

Our confidence is sorely shaken
Our every action seems mistaken
That call we made, the things we said
Oh, how we wish that we were dead
But then we're not, we're just awake
Go back to sleep, for goodness sake

Jazz

His hands, like alligators, are eating up the keys
And he's there, facing the music, jumping up a little on the bench
To pull the notes out of that battered old box
Running up the keyboard to hit the one note that gets you
Left hand laying down the beat for the trumpet to soar over
We're pinned to our chairs and know we can only witness
And take it in

The trumpet now is overstated, but no matter, the moment will pass
And another will come to take its place and then it will be now again
Always now, moving to the next bar, the next inspiration,
One note coming out of the one before it, without thought,
All made from feeling, rising to drive us crazy

Krazy

I am always ready to play along
And trace the picture here before us
Two trees amidst the wilderness
Two birches in the forest

The moon shines down
Through leaf and limb
It's raining down upon us
And sings so sweetly in the dark
To you, Ignatz, Addunniss

You merry mouse
You show yourself
Not through words
But through your actions
With your bricks of love
A house we'll build
A shelter from all factions
Of discord
And of datchord
Of one and
One another
For me, there's you
That's all there is
There isn't any other

Late Morning Call

That little voice next door
Behind the hedge
Independent of all care
Needing no audience
Aware only of its tune and occupation
Studying the grass
Instructing the ants
Training the flowers to grow

And, all the while,
An even flow of sweetness
A song just beyond my reach
I hear her voice
The notes, but not the lyrics
Unnecessary really
Only my curiosity
Has me leaning forward in my chair
She sings on,
Innocent of everything, except
The thread of eager melody
She is following

Unidentified Flying Object

Was that a robin
or
a sparrow?

Automatic Bank Deduction

Go ahead,
take it all!

Mid-life Crisis

Oh, my God,
My hair!
My waistline!
My bank account!
And death, too!

Tricycle

On my fifth birthday
A black and orange three-wheeler
With whitewalls
Magically appeared on the second floor
It took me years to figure out
How it got there

Ignorance

Ignorance may not really be bliss,
But, at least, you don't have to worry
about everything.

Only The Lonely

That sense that joy is our real calling
And that we don't know how to answer

Poetry

This is what I think.
It ain't poetry,
but it gets the feeling right.

The clouds flow toward us
borne on the silver river
of their own bright rain

Little do they know
Or remember
Another time of truth
When magic thought it pleasure to trust

Questions never compelled the story
And old boys, fathers, and friends
Explored this sacred fire
Thinking it essential to create poetry
Beneath the howling clouds and soaring shadows
Showing the stars how to sing
And the ghosts to confess

From *Magnetic Poetry*

Little Leaves

Little leaves
All green and glowing
Translucent, layered
Patient, knowing
Floating, moored
On delicate stems
Beaming there
My little gems
Each one separate
From the others
Still, it's clear
That you are brothers
Connected, yet,
Unique and one
Each with a job
That must be done
To shade
To shine
Or show the way
To sleep at night
To smile by day

Magnetic Poetry

Some of these poems, and others, are written in that wonderful structure provided by Magnetic Poetry. What a process! There you are, looking for the next word and losing your train of thought and then finding yourself going down a road you never knew existed before. Sometimes, dropping the little piece of word and digging it out of the cracks in the floor below you. You get stuck, because you can't find the word you just know is going to make the poem catch fire, but you're forced, by this necessity, to find another way. This is a great way to stretch your brain and search your heart. Imagine the words that follow in that stuttered script, each word separate from the next, as if it's a ransom note. Don't let that scare you. They only want your attention.

Man
What can I say
Grammar is a light in the language we live
But how can you feel the dance
And
See the sky as a precious orchestra
Without giving it all up
And
Write from your heart
Always imagining a game with no death
A sweet dream of life and love
Letting our voices shine
A ferocious and matchless gift

The 1%

Having manacled life and beauty
Old monkeys make us their obedient servants
Curse our kind hearts
Devour our places of grace
Crush the wild water
Kill rob sacrifice those who
Desire the better
And long for an end to secrets
They laugh as they embrace the dead
And
Throw away the universe

Maybe Death Comes First

Maybe death comes first
A heartache that prepares us
For a shining collection of moments
Before something no one knows
No one can imagine

Sometimes death comes first
Before we have the sense
Or any knowledge of ourselves
It shakes our foundation of love
And confuses things
Leaving children, dazed and confused

Death has always come first
Demanding everything, consuming all
No matter what our wishes, our needs
It's a darkness this side of things
It's a fear dissolved only by faith
It's a destination, we think, unreachable,
Impossibly distant

And why is this?
And what comes after?
Better to ask what's here now
After will take care of itself
Our trials and triumphs are
More than enough
To keep us busy

Mendelssohn

The Wedding March is a wonderful tune
Felix composed it in early June
He married a girl in late July
It's December now and he wonders why

He says it was all a Midsummer's Night's Dream
That things are not what they once seemed
His sweetheart then, has now turned sour
Each married minute is like an hour

A carefree man was he
Without words, but full of melody
His way was clear, his problems few
Before he uttered the words "I do."

He ran away to Italy
To learn what happiness could really be
There he became a great sensation
Divorce for him brought reformation

Paper Crowns

We sit here with our paper crowns,
speaking quietly to each other
turning right and turning left
stopping occasionally
reacting
remembering
or lost in a wonder that includes everything —
the delicious light as it comes through the window
the endless day that is passing
the noble company around us
the sad idea that makes us laugh
at ourselves,
there, with our paper crowns

Self-possession *for Caitlin*

Were you ever a young child?
I can't quite picture it
I see you held hostage by Indians,
in Wyoming,
And you telling them that you hope
They are aware of the consequences of this
And that you hold them collectively responsible
For anything you might have missed
During this incredibly difficult time of your life

Snow, Early Morning

Flakes so light, they're not concerned
with what's down below.
Fueled by an internal purpose,
they wiggle their graceful way
around and sideways and back again,
before finally succumbing to inevitable gravity.
Destinations of branch or post or sidewalk
are mere afterthoughts, unavoidable.
Infused with joy and wide awake,
they have their journey
and are making the most of it.

The Dread of Memory

Memory, in itself, is not unkind.
It's the guards in that museum
who make you feel like
you're enjoying yourself too much
or you're speaking too loudly
or you're getting much too close to
things of value.

They might just clear their throat
and give you a look
or they might pointedly remark,
Sir!
Or, if they're having a bad day,
they might just grab you by the arm
and lead you to the side of things
and tell you that your behavior
is particularly atrocious.

You feel bad,
you reassure them that
you'll be better next time
and then,
finally,
it occurs to you to ask yourself
who hired these guys in the first place.

The last time she laughed
A world more difficult than this
Relaxed its haunted form
And let passion flash full
Drunk with the night
Made mad with rhythm

A spirit of glorious amusement filled
Each open heart
With sweet song
So ripe and warm
So soft and deep
That every wild rose could imagine its soul
Changed from ancient dream to new symbol

From *Magnetic Poetry*

The Lottery

The check was no bigger than a normal one
Not the huge facsimile they present you with
At the door, when they try
To milk your luck for their publicity
I had never seen that many zeroes
In one place before

I hoped this bank was big enough
To hold all my money
I wasn't sure what I would do
With all of it
But I was willing to find out

The Potato Polka

When we Scandahoovians sit down to eat
We see our favorite mealtime treat
And we shove aside that slab of meat
That's when we do
The Potato Polka

There is wisdom in those simple wuds
That one must nip things in the buds
But, please sir, spare the spuds
We want to do
The Potato Polka

My girl, it's true, can eat her share
And can't fit into her own chair
But, you see, she doesn't care
Because she's doing
The Potato Polka

Now some will tell you it's potato
And some, they say that it's potaato
But we don't care, we want them pronto
We want to do
The Potato Polka

There's nothing so beautiful as a spud
Though it starts its life beneath the mud
So, let's toast this Goddess with some suds
While we do
The Potato Polka

The Wakeup Call

Asleep in slumber, so far away
The night has ended and now it's day
Time to rise, the breakfast's ready
But all is still, her breathing steady

I call her name, I shake her shoulder
I fear her (No!) but she's getting older
I threaten her and, here, I blunder
She pulls the covers, she's headed under

I try to reason, but that won't succeed
I offer money, but there's no greed
I control myself and act the parent
But her morning speed is too inherent

I cross the hall to appeal to her mother
But she's conked out, I try the brother
He raises his head, but his eyes don't see
They're all asleep, there's only me

Remaining calm, I count to ten
I draw a breath and try again

To the Author

It's tough to fill the empty pages
With all those inky scratches
Like trying hard to start a fire
Without those stinking matches

First one word and then the next
You're building your libretto
It starts out kind of slow at first
And then moves allegretto

The characters begin to speak
Not knowing what to say
But soon you just can't shut them up
They're in each other's way

The scenery is beautiful
You stop and watch it all
Before you know it, spring is gone
And you find that it's late fall

The romance needs attention
To make it really right
It's obvious that they're in love
But all they do is fight

The plot is slowly hatching
So slow it makes you weep
You work it over breakfast
You talk it in your sleep

And then it really starts to move
It's living and it's breathing
You just sit back, it writes itself
You arrive home without leaving

That's what you've been waiting for
When eggs turn into birds
But what a lot of work it was
And what a lot of words

But now it's done, it's finished
It's not like any other
It only took a couple years
Hey, why not write another

True Love

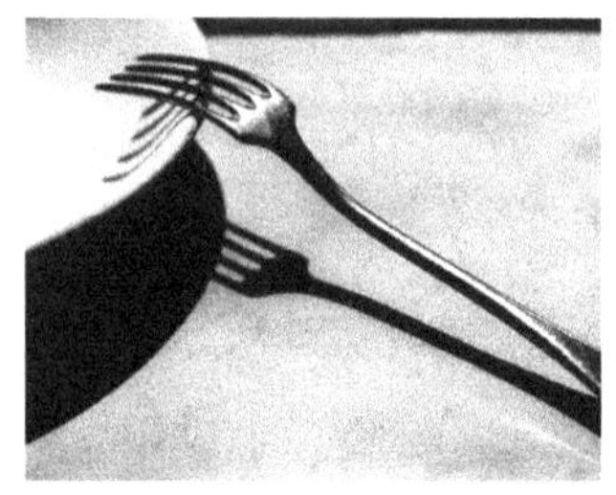

She dropped her fork
and said,
"I can't see you anymore."

Later,
he was heard to remark,
"I'll never use a fork again."

W

In alphabetical organization
There's little room for improvisation
First A then B then C then D
And somewhere in there Q
It's singular in every case
Except the double U

We

We
Are two
Are one
Are we
You the sun
I the sea
In love
With love
With each
Are we
Are two
Are one
Are you
Are me

Where'd It Go?

I woke this morning and all my hair
Had disappeared, it wasn't there
I ran my hand across my dome
But the hairs were gone, no, none at home
I checked the pillow and beneath the sheet
Yet all was white and clean and neat

I went to the bathroom, checked the mirror
The loss could not be shown much clearer
It took no very great detection
To see the blinding light bounce in reflection
From atop my head where all was bare
No mistake, no dream, a real nightmare

I called the cops, I woke my wife
This couldn't really be my life
They gathered round and they inspected
The place from which the hair defected
A desert there, from ear to ear
A desolate, shiny hemisphere

My mind was racing, I couldn't think
My wife came forward with a drink
Orange juice, not Scotch, not beer
For now, of course, the kids were here
No place to hide, I couldn't take it
I knew there'd be no way to fake it
No wig, no toupee, or fancy rug
No remedy, no spell, no helpful drug
No rescue from this mean attack
No way, no how, to bring it back

My wife said, it's true, you are not furry
But really there's no need to worry
I'm sure this happens all the time
It's a natural thing, Dear, not a crime
There are many men who've lost their hair
And they look handsome, dashing, debonair

I wasn't listening, I couldn't hear her
Mortality had come much nearer
My world was changing, my youth was crumbling
What could I do? I stood there mumbling
Minutes passed that seemed like hours
I was afraid I'd lost my manly powers

And then the light broke on me clearly
That though I'd miss those hairs quite dearly
I was still a man, no doubt about it
And all that hair, I'd live without it
I'd face the music, I'd do all that
If only I could find my hat

Whisper we
You and I
Beneath the ferment
Between flood and moon
Every champagne smile in silent shadows
We cry with diamonds for ideas and music for brains
Burning speaking a language too willing to blush
But always asking for a thousand perfect springs
And
Worshiping life as if joy were breath
And eternity finite

From *Magnetic Poetry*

Other Stuff

From the garage, boxes, and notebooks

At the Tip of His Pen (or pencil)

He had a job to do. This was how he liked to think of it. His job was writing. He shied away from considering himself an artist. That was too grand a term, too self-important. Writer, if you didn't think about it too much and said it in a quick, matter-of-fact voice, sounded utilitarian, like farmer or carpenter. And that was not far off the mark, for Norton wrote books of a how-to nature — *How to Bring Out The Best In Your Bulldog, Raising Fish for Fun and Profit, Spot Removing at Home.*

This had proven to be a decent occupation for him, providing a good income and allowing his natural curiosity free rein and eventual satisfaction. There were an infinite number of things to learn, and Norton was worldly enough to know that there were others, beside himself, who would want to learn them, too. Subjects presented themselves as a matter of course.

If his car broke down and he found himself stranded on the side of the road, within moments, the outline had been laid for, *Engine Repair for Non-Mechanics.* If he read an article in the paper about a woman being unfairly evicted from her place of business, he would immediately find himself composing the first paragraph of what would soon become, *Holding Your Own with Landlords.* Or if he found his faucet dripping, before he knew it, the text began forming for, *Life Without Plumbers.*

This how-to-ing and explaining was all very well, but Norton had a desire, which he kept secret from his agent and editor. This was to write a novel of epic proportion and endless familial intrigue. In fact, he had been writing this book for seven years and there was still a lot he had to say.

It was the saga of the Bishop family, a collection of fathers, mothers, uncles, aunts, and children, who, as they exercised their pioneer spirit, also took it upon themselves to make life miserable for each other. The Bishop family was in the process of making their way West across the young continent toward their dreams of wide open spaces, unlimited riches, and power of a raw and naked sort.

Among this vast group of self-servers was a child, pure of heart, who, despite having her hopes repeatedly crushed and her feelings constantly trampled, persevered toward her goal of becoming what she modestly thought of as an angel of mercy, though she was not entirely certain what that might involve.

It was a complicated story. And Norton had been working on it diligently in his spare time, when something very odd and unsettling happened. He had just reached the part where the family had arrived, more or less intact, at the wild end of what was then called, Kansas Territory. They were preparing for an unknown greater than that which they had already faced and, as they waited for their wagon train to depart, by lamplight, firelight, and moonlight, they studied various inspirational texts far into the cold, bitter darkness — *Conestoga Maintenance, Caring For Oxen, Not Caring For Oxen,* and *Living Without Water.*

The angel of mercy whose name, of course, was Angela, was contemplating the heavens from the warmth and comfort of her blankets. She was describing to her diary, and to the reader, her feelings at this crucial moment in her adventures. It was a philosophical, emotional, and sentimental kind of reflection and she was saying to herself, "I hate it when Randolph looks at me that way. One would think he was..." and it was here that both Angela and Norton stumbled.

Neither of them could summon up the appropriate phrase that would describe this Randolph. It wasn't that they were faced with a difficult choice, an embarrassment of riches, and were trying each one out to assess the results; it was rather that they knew the exact word, the perfect and definitive term, but they could not remember it. They knew, with certainty, that there was a word that encompassed and expressed precisely what they wanted, what the situation demanded and deserved, but when they went to write it, they drew a blank. They had a firm grasp of the feeling, but the words were not there. This was more disturbing for Norton than for Angela. After all, he was the writer. Nevertheless, they both fretted over it.

After a few minutes of futile effort, Norton went on with the story. He decided that the word would come to him later and he could then go back and fill it in. But this never happened. Over the next few days, while he was writing and during the ongoing adventures of Angela and her un-supportive family, this same problem kept occurring.

A descriptive phrase for someone's nose was needed and, though the perfect one was on the tip of his pen, Norton could not come up with the words. After a moment, he settled for "button," though he knew that wasn't right. Another time, what was obviously a lengthy shadow of doom became a "long, dark thing." Dinner wasn't inedible; it was "not so hot." And so on, until it became difficult to find the words for the common, everyday objects that populate a story. His characters opened "the large slab of wood with the handle." They crossed "that wool thing on the floor." They ran for cover to get out of the "falling wet stuff."

Norton was alarmed. It began to affect his how-to books, also. It was disturbing to find himself explaining toaster repair in terms of "this do hicky" and "the round curling things." This failing also invaded his life apart from writing. He was stumped on the phone several times and, while he was thinking, the person on the other end kept saying, 'Hello? Hello?,' which didn't make things any easier.

At the restaurant, where, as a creature of habit, he had eaten for fifteen years, he found himself ordering "that hunk of meat with cheese and bread." Stewart, the waiter, looked at him closely to see if he had been drinking and, deciding that he hadn't, diplomatically raised his eyebrows and nodded his head. But then Norton asked for "that red stuff" and Stewart became truly concerned and inquired, in a friendly, yet still serviceable manner, if everything was all right.

"What do you mean, everything?"

"Well, you're acting a bit strange."

Norton heaved one of those big breaths and motioned for Stewart to sit down. Stewart knew then that this was serious because, despite fifteen years of serving Norton and joking and talking with him and even with an annual exchange of Christmas presents, they had never sat at the same table together.

Norton made a motion with his hand, signifying something, and began his story.

"Stewart, did you ever have something happen to you that you just couldn't understand, but you thought you knew everything about?"

"Well," Stewart thought for a moment, "being married."

"I don't mean that. I mean where it seemed completely out of your control?"

Stewart nodded because he didn't want to complicate matters, but he was still thinking about his marriage.

Norton continued. "I'm a writer and I know words, yet, lately, I often can't remember what it is I want to say or what a thing is called."

"Like you're distracted?

"No. I know what it is, I just can't remember the words."

"That is a ... a..." Stewart scratched his head. "A thing that would inconvenience you."

"Not only that, but it's getting worse."

"Have you gone to one of those guys?"

"What guys?"

"The ones who, you know, fix things."

Stewart looked around as if someone else had said that. Norton looked at Stewart. Then they looked at the half-filled restaurant, hoping to find the explanation for the weird behavior that seemed to be affecting them both. Norton shook the thing that holds his hair and went on.

"Stewart, it seems like the whole world is breaking down. Yesterday, I was at the Post Office, and I swear the woman behind the counter had the same problem. I asked her how much and, after a few confused moments, she said I needed the 41-cent piece of paper with the rough edges."

"Wow."

"Wow is right. Have you noticed anything besides our latest, uh, talking thing here that seems un... un..." Norton closed his viewing balls in his search for the word. Finally, he settled for "Unprobable?"

At this, Stewart became frightened. He moved his bottom resting place holder back from the round eating surface and said, "Norton, I think this is out of our... our... our finger limb stubs. It's..." Here, he made a helpless gesture indicating a space that kept growing. "It's..." (He did it again) “than both of us. Perhaps we’re all those lowest-ranked chess pieces being played with by some...”

Stewart shrugged the two knobs below his hearing tubes. It was obvious he was at a loss for those letter combinations that can hold meaning.

Norton looked around, suddenly shivering, and said, “Stewart, this isn’t right. I’ve got a funny feeling, you know? I can’t explain it. It’s something. It’s just something.”

A Life of Mosquitoes

Bite me at your own risk.

I'm going to tell you a frightening story. One that involves blood, hallucinations, disease, and a high whining sound that signals terror to all who hear it. If you are reading this with small children around, please send them out of the room before going any further.

I am originally from Minnesota. The land of 10,000 lakes and about six trillion mosquitoes. They joke that the mosquito is the State Bird, but no one's laughing. My childhood was spent slapping myself silly. They love me. When a mosquito bites me, a welt the size of Texas develops. They seek me out. They don't see me as a person, but as a walking buffet. I've had many encounters with these high-speed vampires. I know they are just trying to survive, but that's hard to remember when they are trying to pierce your flesh.

Questions flood my mind. Why me? Did I offend them in some way? Am I really that sweet? Do they know something I don't? Did I shower today?

It seems that some people are just tastier than others. My younger sister and I are considered delicacies, while my older sister is barely noticed.

As a child, I would lie awake in the dark and listen intently, as that small whine roamed the room. I heard it as it flew by the window on the other side of the room and I tensed as it came closer. Silence was almost worse. I swatted, I crushed, I ground them between thumb and forefinger and, still, they came. No screen was tight enough. No netting worth its weight. My only escape was out on the lake.

My youth was tortured. Sure, Minnesota's winter was cold, but temperature became an abstract concept, a test of manly endurance. In summer, endurance had nothing to do with it. I couldn't grit my teeth or put on a sweater or mittens. I couldn't run. I couldn't hide. When circumstance begins to close in like that, the best thing to do is to go on vacation.

I discovered there were no bugs or humidity worth mentioning in Colorado. I moved immediately. For many years, I was safe and spent many glorious days in the mountains and on the plains. Repellant was a thing of the past. I could lie on the grass and contemplate the clouds with impunity. It was paradise. Not only had I grown up, but I had done what any reasonable Minnesotan would do — move.

All this and, yet, I recently suffered the worst bite of my life. I can't remember the specific bite, but its effects are still with me. I had contracted the deadly West Nile Virus. Symptoms: my body experienced a parade of Hummers driving over me, back and forth, block after block after block. Someone was kind enough to put me to bed. I moaned and groaned. My head ached. Someone or some thing was trying to dig their way out from behind my left eye. A rash developed and spread.

All activity ceased and I slept eighteen hours a day, for two weeks. I called the doctor. He was familiar with stories like mine. He suggested fluids and rest. I couldn't stay awake long enough to get the needed fluids. Resting was no big deal but didn't seem to be doing anything. He told me I would either live or die.

I love western medicine. It's a philosophy, not a science.

Three months later, I thought I was cured. I felt good, had lots of energy, but, then at eleven in the morning, I lay down for a moment and woke up four hours later. It makes you wonder. The good thing is that now I am supposed to be immune (I hope). I've never been able to get a straight answer about that. It would only be fair. Otherwise, I don't think I'd ever leave the house.

I haven't told you about the Mosquito Tornado, but that will have to wait. Now, whenever I see or hear them, it's an effort to restrain myself. My blood pressure rises, a look (that I can't see) comes over my face and I lunge in their direction, teeth snapping dangerously. Vengeance is mine. I'm biting them back. I'm just trying to survive.

Lesson 10

Originality

Not many of our thoughts are objectively original. For example, to use food as an arena, I'm hungry. Or, I think lima beans are unnecessary and taste like cardboard. Someone else has had similar thoughts, but these have a special meaning for you. It is your stomach that is rumbling and your tastebuds that are so offended by the beans.

If you went a bit further and wrote about either thought in more detail, it would become your story. You would write things that weren't apparent to you, before you started. You would surprise yourself with just how accurately and with what gusto you describe those awful beans. **Originality is what comes about through the act of explanation and description.** These explanations and descriptions are filtered through the unique sensibility and experience each of us possesses.

Many times our thoughts are jumbled and indistinct, but the act of writing or typing necessitates an ordering of those thoughts and, through that act, they can acquire coherence and a definite existence. They appear. We can read them. They are externalized. Whether it is the explanation of what went wrong at the police station or a bit of dialogue between Susan and her mother-in-law, or an inspiration for getting your character off the couch and onto the balcony outside his girlfriend's apartment, these things come from you.

They emerge from the unconscious which is full of loose facts, unrelated observations, and a lifetime of impressions, feelings, and experiences. In the act of writing, we call on our unconscious to come up with these things. To the degree to which we trust it and have faith in it, it will come through for us. Each time we write and have the experience of creating situations and characters and dialogue, our trust and faith is confirmed and strengthened. We know it works. It's there in black and white.

Often, we look at what we have written and wonder, just who did that? **We wonder if we can ever possibly do it again. The answer is yes.** What is true is that there is an infinite amount of material at hand. A whole lifetime of experiences and imagination and a whole world that surrounds you at every moment. You can draw on this experience and this world whenever you like. However, it doesn't happen without effort and intention. You can't just think about it, you have to actually sit down and pick up the pen or turn on your computer and start writing. It is this action that will bring everything out into the open.

Beyond the act and the intention, you need a direction. If you have an idea for a story, then you have a place to start. But you need to start each day, each page, each paragraph. If you don't know where to start, look around or look inside. Could you describe a friend — her appearance, her nature, her history, or the scene last night at the bar, or how it felt driving down 28th Street? Each of these will lead you somewhere. The important thing is that you are writing and, when you are writing, something is happening.

The lessons and exercises in this course are an attempt to provide direction. They get you going. They help you explore specific issues. They develop your writing muscles, so that you can apply them and your energy to your own ends. So that you can pursue and explore the issues that are close to your own heart.

Ideas are everywhere. They are walking down the street. They are on page eleven of the newspaper. They stare back at us from a phrase in the second paragraph we wrote in response to Exercise Four. They emerge from our worries, our hopes, our dreams.

The question arises, am I saying something original? Unless you are copying a passage written by someone else, yes! Everything comes through you. Many stories have the same plot of boy meets girl, but every one is different. Many stories have the same setting — the wild and wooly West, a domestic arrangement, Los Angeles, outer space, yet they are of unlimited variation.

Everyone has a story to tell. Many stories, if they choose to tell them. Don't worry about saying something new or that what you say must be completely different or completely original. Don't be dismayed if the idea in your head seems somewhat plain and simplistic. When you actually fit the pieces together and have described it and provided incident and action, you will find that your story stands on its own. It is a story. You wrote it and no one else could have written it in the same manner or with the same effect.

Our work is original because we are. We have only to begin, to find out what it is we have to say. Work hard. Don't worry. Have fun. The words are all there. We just have to write them down.

Exercise –

Every exercise is an opportunity to see that you are full of original thought, original detail, and interesting things to say. Do each one of the following and then read them over. You will see that you have pulled the rabbit out of the hat. Before, your paper or screen was blank. Now there is something on it. Something that came from you. Something original.

1. Describe the street or road you grew up on.
2. Tell me about your first experience of driving a car.
3. Who is a hero of yours and why?
4. Write a dialogue, in which something is asked for and denied.

— From *Ringer's Secret School of Writing — Semester Two*

Coin of the Realm

My great-grandfather originally came from Poland. In the 1870s, Russia invaded Poland and drafted him into the Imperial Guard. He was drafted because he was very handsome and because he was six feet, four inches tall. Also, because the Czar needed troops to strengthen his rule. Everyone called my great-grandfather, Pup.

So, he went to Russia. One of his assignments was to guard the Imperial throne room. It was in this room that the Czar held court and dispensed the justice required of him as the head of state. The room was huge. Built on a scale that dwarfed even Great-grandfather. It held a long colonnade with windows high up, through which the pale light shone. It was lit by torchlight, but the ceilings were high enough that smoke was never a problem.

At first glance, it seemed a dark, dreary, and lonely place, as indeed it was. But when the court was there, bright colors would dance between the columns, jewels would shine and reflect the flickering torches that burned night and day. The red velvet of the throne became the focal point of the room as everyone awaited the Czar's appearance. Great-grandfather, Pup, stood rigid at one side of the throne, staring nowhere and watching everything. He loved this room and, though drafted, he came to love the Czar he had been forced to serve.

One day, he was on duty alone in the great hall. No one was expected, but the throne was guarded at all times. Pup, who was a young man at this time, was possessed with a great desire to sit on the throne, just once. It was a curiosity which he had never admitted before and which seized him suddenly. He turned his head slowly and slightly to each side to make sure he was alone. He quietly lay down the rifle that was slung from his shoulder.

As he stood in front of the throne, facing an imaginary court, he placed his hands over the ends of the carved arms shaped like talons grasping a globe. His grip tightened. He drew his breath and, with his back straight, sank onto the throne. He had been there but a moment, when a voice from the darkness behind him sent a chill down his spine. The voice, disembodied yet commanding, asked, "How do you like it?" Pup could not move though he knew his life was in jeopardy. A tall figure strode into the faint light. Again, the voice demanded, "How do you like it?" Great-grandfather then recognized the Czar.

Pup shook as he rose and answered, "Your Highness, it affords me little rest." The Czar looked at him, smiled thinly, and replied, "Nor for me." As he said this, Pup picked up his rifle and returned to his duty. He dared not look at the Czar. But the Czar came near and placed a silver coin into his hand, saying, "Guard me well, as I try to protect you also." In a moment he was gone. Pup was once again alone with the lights, the throne, and a coin of the realm.

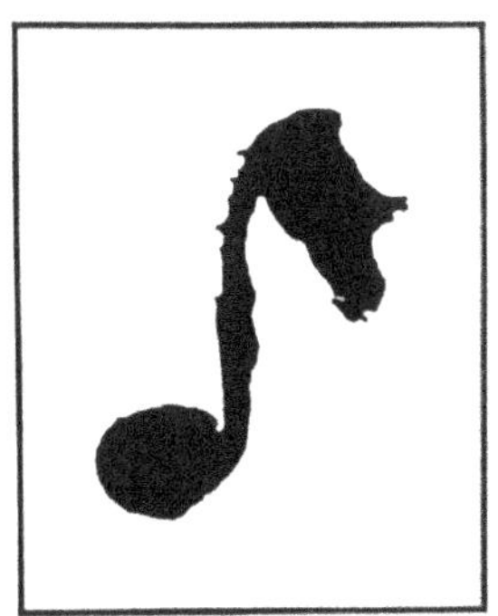

Music — A melodious part of our daily requirements.

Music soothes the savage beasts and savages, like you and me. The wonderful thing about it is its infinite nature. There exist tons of music of every type, manner, and description. I wouldn't dare begin to describe it. But being infinite in nature, there is no store that can hold it all. Not even, Amazon. And, it goes without saying, that no one mind, nor even the cumulative mind of an entire, blindly dedicated Glee Club can know it all. It's a gift to have someone recommend something you've never heard and could never imagine. It's fun to discover something that is new. And, if music be the food of love, let the feast begin!

There are so many tunes, records, CDs, etc. that I love. You might like them. You might not. Each is an invitation to another place, and sometimes, another time. We see what moves us, we rock out, and, as the King once said, Keep the Hi-fi high and the lights down low. Play on, you heroes. Play on.

Introduction to Tales of the Vampire Hunters

Sometimes, things are not what they seem. That sweet looking grandma, next to you at the movies, may just be waiting for the lights to dim before she sinks her hideous fangs into your neck during the previews. That upstanding political figure you see daily on TV might have a nightlife that would shock and appall you. Anyone could be one of them, whether by choice or, initially, against their will. Possession has no favorites: innocent looking bus drivers, college professors, plumbers, nurses, florists, postal workers, house cleaners, golf pros, waitresses, bank tellers, top chefs, financial advisors, even siblings, uncles, and distant cousins.

Sometimes, I wonder if any of us is safe. Vampires, zombies, demons, and creatures of the night are everywhere – in libraries waiting for lights out, at the mom and pop on the corner, in bike lanes, near health clubs, behind those bushes. It's amazing anyone goes out at night.

I'm not telling you anything you didn't know before. I just want you to be on the alert, aware of what might take you down, at any moment, like the big water buffalo you are. I want to caution you against complacency and warn you, once again, that they can be anywhere and, by all accounts, are growing in numbers that should scare us all.

Fortunately, we have heroes and defenders, who have been with us throughout the ages. The fact that any of us dare to venture forth in the darkness owes much to these brave souls who have, at great personal expense and self-sacrifice, dedicated their lives to seeking out and defending the rest of us. Defending us from a fate that was once a quite rare (and immediately hushed up) occurrence in some eastern European hamlet, surrounded by huge dark forests, sharp mountains, and strange music. A fate that now is commonplace, an ever-present danger that menaces both large urban areas and suburban havens, formerly safe from this sort of thing.

Whether one calls them Vampire Hunters, Demon Hunters, or even the newly popular, Zombie Killers, we can thank them for what safety still remains. Their vigilance and refusal to accept defeat should inspire us all. This is a testament and shout out to their noble calling and fearless actions. Without them, nothing would be as it is. Join me in celebrating their achievements.

Ernest Hemingway, Demon Hunter

Ernest Hemingway was a humorless man. But he was a clever one. He wrote many stories. Some were longer than others. He liked to hunt and he killed what he liked. This did not help his humor. He was loved by many women but could not love them back. He romanticized many things and was a survivalist. War was in his nature. Truth was in his heart. His beard was on his face.

Once, in Barcelona, he met a man. They shared a few drinks. They argued late into the night, which was a sure sign of Hemingway's friendship. In a haze of conviviality, the man leaned toward Hemingway, who thought he was about to be kissed. Shocked, H stood up abruptly and upset the table with their drinks. He didn't see the sly smile on the man's face, as he went quickly out the door.

This incident, though treated as a joke by H's buddies, bothered him more than it should have. A sense of humor might have helped at this point. But, as you know, that was like wishing for rain, in a dry country.

Several days later, while attending a party, Hemingway saw this same man on the other side of a room. Their eyes met and, this time, H saw that smile. He confronted the man, who said he only wanted to get to know him better. Hemingway said, "How much better?" The man answered, "Let me show you a little trick."

By this time, several partygoers were looking on. The man moved his hands, like a magician, and following these, Hemingway was taken by surprise, as the man suddenly, but gently, leaned over and bit his neck. H reflexively raised his hand to the site of the bite. When he brought it down, everyone could see the blood. He started to say something, in an immoderate tone, but the man had vanished.

H looked round, the victim of this urbane, but hideous creature. H was red and furious. He tried to make a joke to the people gathered there, but, of course, the joke fell flat. He said, "That Dracula son of a bitch!"

At the time, he didn't know how close to the truth he was. Though he gave no sign, he made a vow in that moment, to find and kill the man who had so completely scared and humiliated him. This was how Hemingway, now haunted by this mysterious and, somehow, erotic encounter, became known not only as a celebrated writer, defined by his own ideas of masculinity, but also a dedicated and persistent Demon Hunter. His nights would never be the same again.

Indeed, many years later, in Idaho, desperately tired of the campaign he had waged against the Demons for so long, and losing his will, he famously took his own life. Hunters come and go, but the creatures of the night, eternally on the prowl and dashing, in their own way, continue to disturb and taunt mankind throughout the ages.

— From *Tales of the Vampire Hunters*

Lately

Lately… whatever that means. It could mean, for the past several months, or for the last week or so, or for the last couple of days. If one factors in the Information Revolution, aging, and the possible onset of that disease whose name I can never remember, it could be this morning or just a minute ago.

However, it may be that lately, I've been experiencing myself in a new way. I mean experiencing myself not in the biblical sense, but that my actions, thoughts, and feelings are all in alignment and working together.

There is an identifiable sense of self.

This sense of self may strike you as something that should be obvious, or something to be worked out in the second year of college, or something completely incomprehensible. To me, it is something willfully created, struggled for, hoped for, but which can only come about in its own time. I have been looking for this switch, with determination, through the years and have never found it.

I always tried to be whoever they wanted me to be — good son, well-behaved student, businessman, employee, but I could never really get the hang of it. I spoke inappropriately. My biorhythms were out of sync. I worked too much or not enough. I knew I was not fulfilling my potential. I was not buckling down to the job at hand. I was not taking the whole thing seriously.

I tried but, inevitably, each time, I would fail. I was like an incurable alcoholic. I had, with shame, hidden some facet of myself in the bottom desk drawer. I had a couple of those small airplane bottles of longing, stuffed behind my socks. I kept saying I would quit but never could. The voices in my head were too insistent, too distracting.

I had to face the truth: I was an imposter. A sheep in wolf's clothing. An emperor with no clothes. A guy who hadn't done the laundry. Metaphors popped up unbidden. Bad puns disturbed perfectly reasonable sentences. My visions were not remotely similar to the Strategic Marketing Plan. I was a cause of disappointment to my parents.

An object of worry to my sisters. A failure in the eyes of my friends. And, I was unemployable.

This left me with few options. There would be no title — Captain of Industry — for me. I would not figure in the Alumni News. I would never become a CPA. Somewhere, back there, I had my Occupational Aptitude tested and, though it was exciting to contemplate, I knew, even then, that I would never become a television repairman or an astronaut. I'm afraid of heights.

Now what?! This is a question I repeatedly asked myself. And that was exactly the problem. Me and myself were on different sides of the fence. I could not figure it out and, myself, try as it might, couldn't make me hear the answer. In many ways, time (in general), age (in particular), the state of the world, and the economy, wore me down. I gave up all of my ambiguous ambitions. It seemed as if every possibility had been exhausted or wasn't interested. To continue the metaphor from before, I gave up and said, dejectedly, 'Make it a double and keep 'em coming.'

But metaphors are only that. They break down at some point and it's hard to keep things straight. Are we talking about philosophy, psychology, or psychosis? Does drink represent desire or de-opposite?

What has happened is one of those ironies, upon which many major religions have been founded: Surrender to what is and peace will follow. Stop looking and you will find it. Wherever you go, there you are.

The only thing to do has been to take the advice of the masters — Turn off your mind, relax, and float downstream. Go with the flow. Turn, turn, turn. Keep on truckin.' It seems those guys in the sixties were on to something.

Lately… I've just been trying to do my best.

A Song

Vic was beaming in a fixed way, as he continued, "Gus is going to sing a little tune for your dining and dancing pleasure called, *'Every Night Is Saturday Night for Me.'* "

In the West
The sun burns bright and shiny
And the horizon is far away
But it's the same the whole world over
The night always follows the day

When the sun goes down and darkness falls
The stars are a sight to see
But they can't compare to this feeling I have
Every night is Saturday night for me

Every night is a time for singing
And love is the dominant key
I'll worry tomorrow morning
It's Saturday night for me

So what if it's only Tuesday
And I have troubles from A to Z
I'll feel delight by the end of the night
It's Saturday night for me

Every night is Saturday night for me
I won't mope around and
Wear a big frown
I'll head downtown and
I won't sit down, because
Every night is Saturday night for me

The band ended the song with a flourish and the crowd, such as it was, went wild. These were sentiments that they thoroughly understood.

— From *Gus Goes West*

Oh, Earthlings

When walking over a bridge, say, a rope bridge that sways in the breeze, it's much less difficult (and more fun) if you aren't concentrating on each step or on getting to the other side. You could check out the view. If you are questioning your balance and calculating the distance you might fall, you're tormenting yourself with real and imagined failures from the past. This makes it both difficult and painful.

Stick to the plan. Bring yourself back to the plan. Don't require success at every moment or demand that your state of mind always be at its highest pitch. That will signal (convincingly, but falsely) irreparable inadequacy.

Do what you can, when you can. Conserve the dazzle for when it's really needed. Ask for and seek help from wherever it may be available. Don't succumb to destructive and distracting fatigue and fear. None of that will or can help you.

Exercise the strength and knowledge you've developed through hard won experience. Remain grateful and sensitive to what is happening at this moment. Be aware of what's around you as you take each step forward, each breath that sends you energy, the line of the horizon where green meets blue, the distinct sound of the bird perched somewhere nearby. Breathe with conscious recognition of the magic involved in this accustomed act.

Rest, eat, move. Don't give aid or comfort to the fears that are begging for your company. Stick to the plan. Study the plan. Add to or adjust the plan. Expand it. Refine it. Realize that this is what your soul, your unconscious, your solid self has assembled as what is needed, what is essential to move you forward. Trust it and make use of it.

Live long and prosper, Earthling.

Calendars

The Days of Our Lives

What constitutes a long time? Let me count the days. No, forget it. That's too difficult. Just counting the years gives me pause.

A calendar is a useful tool, an incremental celebration, a place of record for important dates — bills due, dentist appointments, daylight savings reminders. It's a mental assistant for those of us with short-term memory loss, a bunch of boxes on a piece of paper, a black and white matrix imposed on us by some obscure Roman emperor, and, in my case, an excuse to have some pictures on the wall.

This is the 25th anniversary edition of the Ringer Calendar. I have been producing these calendars since the age of seven. Go ahead, you calculators. That means I'm thirty-two. To some of you, that might seem young. But these bleary eyes have seen every one of those days. This has given me the perspective and confidence to know that one year always follows another.

In that spirit of inevitable anticipation and hope, I wish you all the best in the coming New Year. Let the bubbles begin! With hearts beating, lift your glasses, see eye to eye, and toast each other and every minute we have together in this wonderful world.

* There were thirty years of Ringer Calendars. These are a sample of the covers.

1982
CALENDAR

THE 1984
RINGER
CALENDAR

THE 1986 RINGER CALENDAR

THE 1988 RINGER CALENDAR

10th ANNIVERSARY EDITION

Upcoming Publications

The Search for
Nowhere

It's around here somewhere.

Ted Ringer

Bestselling author of
The Cat's Out of The Bag
[illegible]

16 Tons
of Cheesecake

A Fable

Translated from the French
by
Ted Ringer

Don't Try to Reason
with Me.
I'm going anyway.
by Ted Ringer
author of The Long Highway

If 6 Were 9,
I Would Have Graduated
By Now.
Ted Ringer
Author of
Speeling Isn't Everything

Honey, They're Back!
WE HAD WAITED SO LONG. NOW, WE WOULD FINALLY LEARN WHAT WE NEEDED TO KNOW.
Ted Ringer

Just like last summer!
LET'S TWIST
AGAIN!
TED RINGER

Pictures

There is nothing like a bone
Nothing in the world
There is nothing you can own
That is anything like a bone

You know, we're not getting any younger.

Cocktail Hour

I have a little headache.

Knocking Myself Out.

The Statue of Normality

The Hell of Neckties

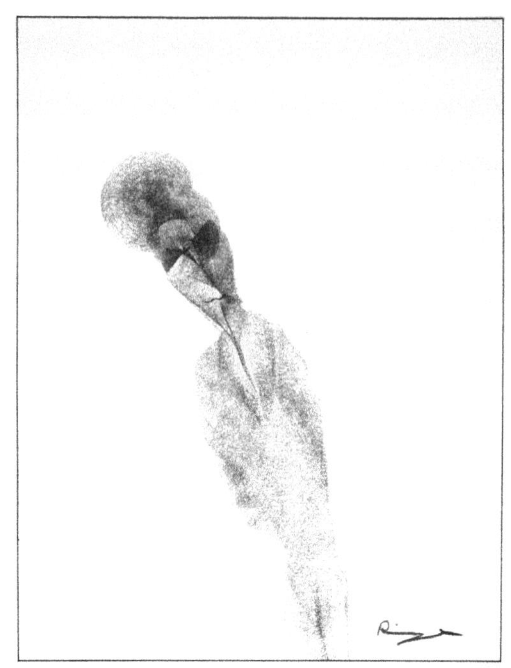

SECRET AGENT MAN

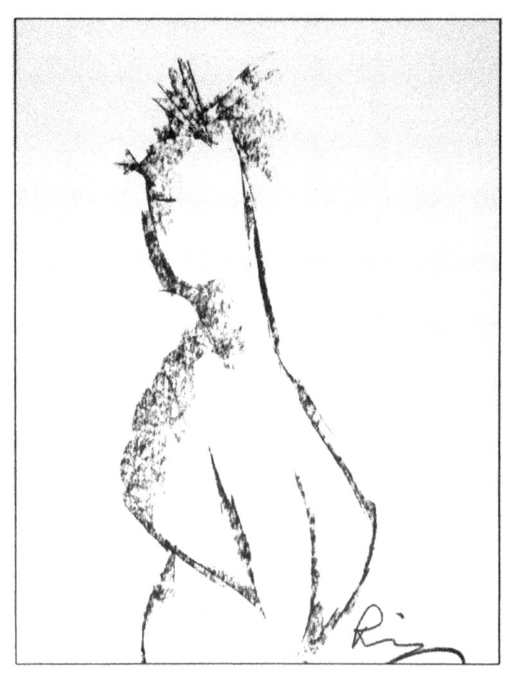

FLAMENCO DANCER

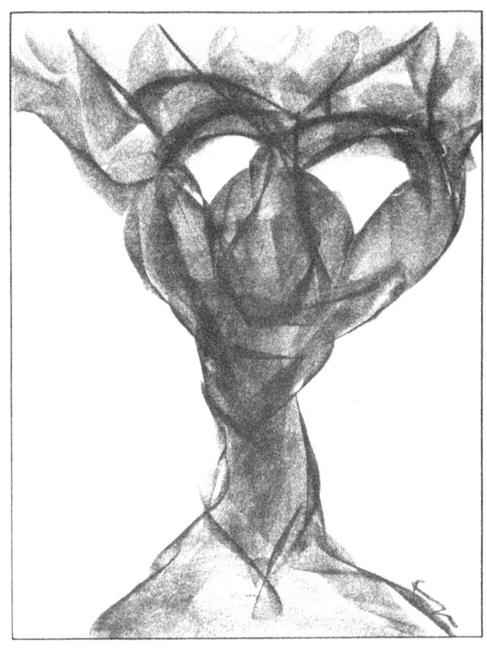

THE ALIEN

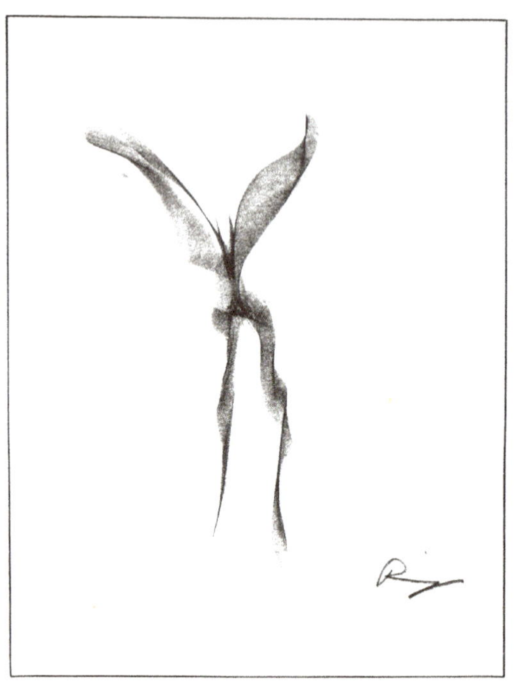

The Devil

BeeBop

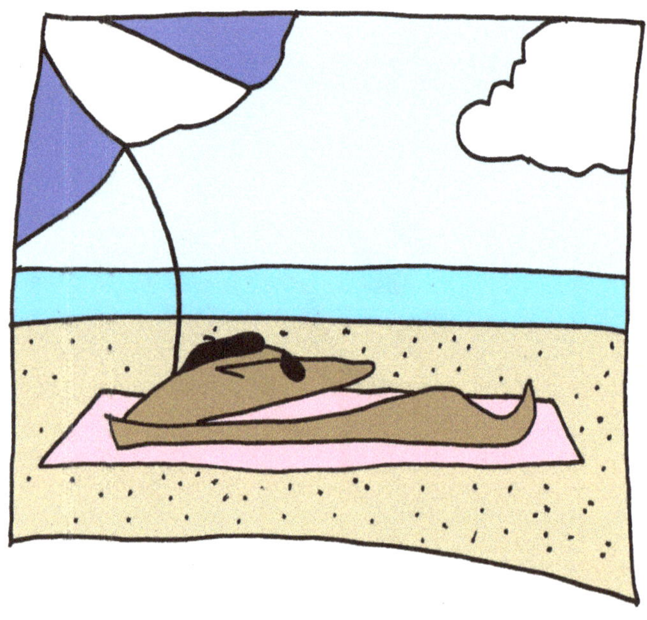

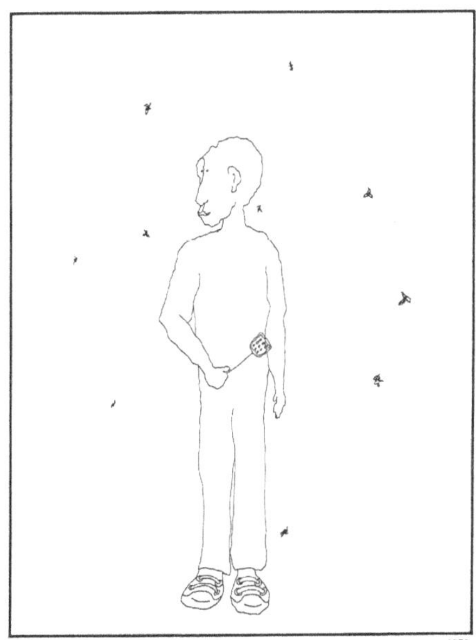

1978

Lord of the Flies.

Child of Adult Acne.

The Conversation.

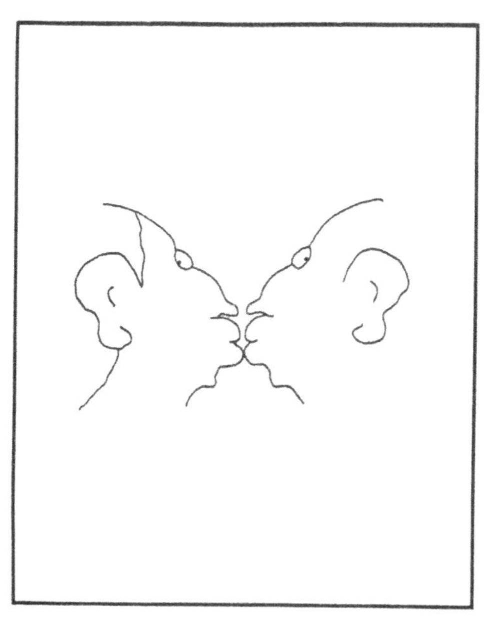

I measure success in donuts.

www.bumpersticker.guru

Family Cartoons

Our Motto —Always enough. Never too Much.

I'm experiencing a lot of surface tension.

I must have confused self-help with help yourself.

It's mental,
incremental.

As a kid, I went to camp
in Roswell.

Multi-tasking
always ends in tears.

There we were, all of us,
on the head of the same pin.

An institution?
They'd be lucky to have me.

Proof of insurance?
I'm broke, aren't I?

No, seriously,
I'm kidding.

Where there's a hill,
there's a way around it.

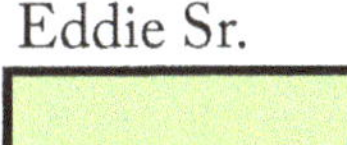

Ted Ringer

Back in the day,
I wanted to reach out
and get a tattoo.

Eddie Sr. Ted Ringer

In my case, a life of the
mind is confusing.

I haven't been this hot
since Disco.

In the War Between the States,
I picked South Dakota.

Ask me about
my acid trips!

My Zen drink —
no glass, no ice, no olive.

Grow up, while you can.

Mom, am I a butterfly
dreaming I'm a baby?

I can’t be trusted with money.

Daycare gets me out of the house.

When I grow up,
I'll have my own couch.

My favorite musical is
Guys and Dogs.

Is the bowl half empty
or half full?

Leash or Lasso of Oppression?

To you, it's barking.
To me, it's poetry.

Mom always said, don't run
with the pack.

Obedience isn’t everything.

One cupcake is never enough.
Never!

I'm pushing the envelope
and adding two stamps!

When I wish upon a star,
I don't hold back!

I bring out the best in me!

And in the end…

What are we going to do? It is what it is. The hard-earned wisdom that we now possess tells us this is a cause for both celebration and gratitude, a time for lifting our glasses to the Universe and the hard-working people in it, and a time for barging around laughing, as we encounter, inevitably, but also at just the right moment, that good, good, night.

Acknowledgments

There are many people who have helped me along the way of this book. And along the way of things in general. Specifically, I want to thank Dianna North, Carolyn Oakley, Russell McDougal, Polly Leftofsky, Valari Jack, George Peters, Ashley Thoth, Lucia Newell, Steve Wiese, Dan Schumann, and W. S. Sutton for their friendship, assistance, hard work, and fun.

Wonderful World Publishing Company

www.ingramcontent.com/pod-product-compliance
Lightning Source LLC
Chambersburg PA
CBHW050024040726
47599CB00015B/1532

* 9 7 8 0 9 8 4 8 8 0 7 1 3 *